Part imagined intimate diary of the poet Rubén Darío, part lyrical exploration of the rich inner life of poet Aragón, this pulsating book is an ode to the between-world of those who live a life dedicated to observation of words. Sonically charged lines that delve into solitude, travel, separation, grief, and the complex life of the outsider allow these poems to speak both to the individual Latinx experience and the universal desire to belong, to be heard.
—**Ada Limón**, author of *The Carrying* and *Bright Dead Things*

Consider all of this / an excursus on origins," advises Francisco Aragón as he invites the reader into the queer Latinx literary lineage in *After Rubén*. Comprised of equal parts familial and scholarly figures and conflicts, the depiction of Rubén Darío's poetic legacy in this collection reveals his lasting impact on Aragón, whose verse illuminates a range of complex and passionate lives. Aragón's translations (the originals are reproduced in an appendix) and ekphrastic re-visions of ten of Darío's poems are daring and, indeed, "blasphemous."
—**Carmen Giménez Smith**, author of *Cruel Futures* and *Be Recorder*

After Rubén es una maravilla. Its elegant, lapidary poems are whispered, intoned, delivered like manifestos, or sung in halting measures that transmute the ephemera of memory and witness into the flashes and trails of glimpsed truths. Francisco Aragón, an American poet of uncommon ambition, has created a bejeweled puzzle box of a book, a fragmented Mariposa memoir of a childhood in between worlds, set within an homage to the poets whose inspirations helped him find his voice, all of which is interwoven in a celebration, an elegy—an interrogation—of the legacy of his greatest literary "mentor," the great Nicaraguan poet Rubén Darío. In this heady poetic idiom, bridging his home in San Francisco and scenes in Nicaragua with other places from his life in the States, Aragón's poetry hearkens again to the possibility of a poetics of las Americas, unbounded, unabashedly literary across cultures, languages, history, and journalism, unafraid to anatomize itself, and to regard and report the ever-shifting totalities of our Latinidad.
—**John Phillip Santos**, author of *Places Left Unfinished at the Time of Creation* and *The Farthest Home Is in an Empire of Fire*

What is remarkable about this book is Aragón's "here, there, how" ("Canción")—the integration of history, identity, geography, homage, poetry, and prose that characterizes the collection. What contemporary Latinx poetry does best is defy division, instead affirming the complex and beautifully profound communion of beings pulsing through the poet's veins. "I am large," wrote Whitman, "I contain multitudes." This book embodies these words as a powerful argument for justice, compassion and love.
—**Valerie Martínez**, author of *Each and Her*, Poet Laureate of Santa Fe, NM (2008–2010)

also by
Francisco Aragón

Poetry

His Tongue a Swath of Sky (chapbook)
Glow of Our Sweat
Puerta del Sol
Tertulia (chapbook)
In Praise of Cities (chapbook)
Light, Yogurt, Strawberry Milk (chapbook)

Translations

From the Other Side of Night
Sonnets to Madness and Other Misfortunes
Of Dark Love
Body in Flames
Lorca: Selected Verse (cotranslator)
Federico García Lorca: Collected Poems (cotranslator)

Editions

OCHO #15
The Wind Shifts: New Latino Poetry
Dánta: A Poetry Journal, #1 & 2
Mark My Words: Five Emerging Poets
Berkeley Poetry Review, #23/24

AFTER RUBÉN

poems + prose

Francisco Aragón

 Red Hen Press | *Pasadena, CA*

Book design by Mark E. Cull
Cover Art: "Momotombo on Lake Managua" by José Rodeiro,
oil-on-linen, 24"x37," 1995
http://www.rodeiro-art.com

Library of Congress Cataloging-in-Publication Data

Names: Aragón, Francisco, author.
Title: After Rubén : poems / Francisco Aragón.
Description: First edition. | Pasadena, CA : Red Hen Press, [2020]
Identifiers: LCCN 2019027781 (print) | LCCN 2019027782 (ebook) | ISBN 9781597098571
(trade paperback) | ISBN 9781597098168 (ebook)
Classification:LCCPS3601.R34A62020(print)|LCCPS3601.R34(ebook)|DDC811/.6—dc23
LC record available at https://lccn.loc.gov/2019027781 | LC ebook record available at https://
lccn.loc.gov/2019027782

The National Endowment for the Arts, the Los Angeles County Arts Commission, the Ahmanson
Foundation, the Dwight Stuart Youth Fund, the Max Factor Family Foundation, the Pasadena
Tournament of Roses Foundation, the Pasadena Arts & Culture Commission and the City of Pasa-
dena Cultural Affairs Division, the City of Los Angeles Department of Cultural Affairs, the Audrey
& Sydney Irmas Charitable Foundation, the Kinder Morgan Foundation, the Meta & George
Rosenberg Foundation, the Allergan Foundation, the Riordan Foundation, Amazon Literary Part-
nership, and the Mara W. Breech Foundation partially support Red Hen Press.

Publication of this book is made possible in part by support from the Institute for Scholarship in
the Liberal Arts, College of Arts and Letters, University of Notre Dame.

First Edition
Published by Red Hen Press
www.redhen.org

Printed in Canada

para ti, papá

QEPD /RIP

CONTENTS

III

IV

V

Appendix

Ten poems by Rubén Darío

AFTER RUBÉN

¡Oh Momotombo ronco y sonoro! Te amo

—Rubén Darío
Canto errante

You are dead and the dead are very patient.

—Jack Spicer
After Lorca

FOREWORD

by Michael Dowdy

At the crossroads of its *equis*, Latinx poetry gathers worlds upon worlds—tongues, triumphs, and hardships. We're fortunate to encounter in *After Rubén* an expert guide. With joy, pluck, and a warm hand, he takes us to meet his people. His mother, "head brimming with phrases" in English, amulets for escaping the sweatshop. His father, "portly, sugar / in his blood, a whiff of something // on his breath as he speaks / of the Sacramento / River." A sister, her voice "sturdy as the metal / table and chairs / in the patio." Cities north and south, where numina float and settle, "as if a place—León, / Granada—could speak, / whistle, inhabit / a timbre." A Nicaraguan woman testifying about the Contra War, whose words "gather and huddle / in [his] throat." Scoundrels, alas, like Joe Arpaio—"we've caught a glimpse / in the jowls of your sheriff: / bulldog who doubles as your heart." And, in rapture, the poets who sing in his ears and in the poems in our hands.

Francisco Aragón has collected in *After Rubén* several lifetimes of a life in letters. From the "short / skinny boy" with a skateboard and "books in [his] backpack," to the man in a hotel mirror who's come to resemble his father, the constant is poetry. A poet fierce and vulnerable, wizened and empowered by his experiences as a gay Latinx man. A generous advocate for other poets, who share our air or breathe within poems we share with others. *After Rubén* meditates on family, both inherited and made, through filiation, through the words of living and dead. Our guide animates his dead, for, as he writes, "the dead are very patient."

The Rubén of the title is, of course, the Nicaraguan poet Rubén Darío (1867–1916). Rubén—innovator of Latin American *modernismo*, not to be confused with Anglo-American modernism. Darío—recently outed queer poet whose poems Aragón reinvents. Rubén—beating heart of the collection, a body of poems and poets in communion across space and time. Consider the line just above. Borrowed from Jack Spicer's book *After Lorca*, it serves as epigraph to *After Rubén* and the final line of "January 21, 2013," perhaps the book's boldest poem.

Aragón's poems frequently carry dates, marking personal and historical events. The event in "January 21, 2013" unfolds in layers. An epistle in Darío's voice, the poem is addressed to the Nicaraguan writer Sergio Ramírez. His novel, *Margarita, está linda la mar* (1998), takes its title from a Darío poem. Although Rubén rates the novelist's depictions of *his* life, they're not the occasion for Rubén-Francisco's letter. In 2012, Aragón informs us, Arizona State University acquired a privately-held collection of Darío's papers, including nine letters addressed to Mexican poet Amado Nervo, the last of which confirms Darío's love affair with Nervo in *fin-de-siècle* Paris. For reasons that seem clear enough, Ramírez published an essay denouncing the letters as counterfeit, a specious claim refuted by scholars. Speaking from beyond the grave, Rubén tells Sergio, *it's all true.*

The title references Barack Obama's second inauguration, where the Cuban-American Richard Blanco became the first Latinx and openly gay poet to read an inaugural poem. That makes at least six poets figuratively gathered *on* and *in* "January 21, 2013"—Lorca, Spicer, Darío, Nervo, Blanco, Aragón— not counting other poets with cameos in *After Rubén*: Cardenal, Whitman, Herrera . . . Here, Aragón is spirit guide, conduit, time-traveling party host. As Rubén says to Sergio (here, we're on a first-name basis; Eliot and Pound can have their surname-monuments): "Perhaps you're surprised by this letter? / You shouldn't be. Anything is possible / in this racket of ours."

Another type of racket, noise, subtly introduces *After Rubén*, with the poet traveling on BART (Bay Area Rapid Transit). A modified list poem squeezed into a loose, unpunctuated sonnet, "2012" compresses a year of culture— books, journals, playbills—in our poet's life. Is he moving cities, apartments? No matter. This is poetry in motion, on West Coast-East Coast (San Francisco/D.C.), north-south (Indiana/Nicaragua), and transatlantic trajectories (Madrid, Paris, London). Darío, too, was a man in transit. Although he lived in Chile for two years, Nicanor Parra wrote that Darío was one of the three best *Chilean* poets. This is what Aragón and Latinx poetry *do*. They *move*, transgressing nations, languages, selves.

Among the possessions in "2012" are photos and cassettes of Aragón's sister's and father's voices. Throughout *After Rubén*, dynamic interplay unfolds between sight and sound. An elegy to a sister asks what might be put to Darío: "Was recording // you a way of / releasing you?" In English and Spanish, the ekphrastic poem "Photo, 1945"/"Foto, 1945" studies the poet's grandfather and young mother in Managua. The opening tercets foreshadow violence to come. They also stage how seeing *sounds* differently in each language:

The only photo of you, black and white	La única foto de ti, en blanco y negro
and torn—the frayed edge	y rota—el borde desgastado
climbing your chest, just missing	escalando tu pecho, rozando
your left eye, cutting	tu ojo izquierdo, cortando
off your ear: only your face	tu oreja: solo tu cara
was spared. [...]	se salvó. [...]

While this poem of apostrophe subtly interweaves the personal and political, others dramatize the stakes for Latinx lives during an era of anti-immigrant nativism. In *After Rubén*, the poet of *Puerta del Sol* (2005) and *Glow of Our Sweat* (2010) has become more political, joining other contemporary poets of social engagement.

Aragón follows this strand of the poetry of the Americas with a tensile rewriting of Darío's "A Roosevelt" (1904). "To George W. Bush" hews to its spirit, diction, and mode of address, though Aragón torques, tightens, and condenses Darío's poem into enjambed couplets. Bush is "one part wily astute / animal, three parts owner // of a ranch." The ten Darío poems Aragón approximates in English appear in the appendix, where we notice arresting visual differences. Aragón's propulsive version consummates Darío's prophecy for the twentieth century: "Eres los Estados Unidos, / eres el futuro invasor / de la América [Latina]."

Alas, disdain for Latinx and Latin American lives persists. The Trump catastrophe punctuates *After Rubén* in "Keough Hall" and "Helen Speaks." As "January 21, 2013" shows, Aragón's persona poems sparkle. Reading the title "Helen Speaks," I expected *the* Helen (of Troy, whose beauty launched a thousand ships). I conjured Darío's swan, that avatar of *modernismo,* Yeats's "Leda and the Swan," Zeus . . . Instead, *this* Helen is a working-class white woman from northern Indiana, a waitress married to a Latino deported to Mexico after seventeen years of marriage, their children distraught, helpless. *This* Helen, a Trump voter, stares in her mirror, "sit[ting] in the dark / peopl[ing] the wall of [her] sorrow," aghast at the war she's launched.

In this urgent book, and in urgent times, *after* Rubén has many meanings: *temporal* (i.e., following Darío); *homage* (praising Darío); *inspiration* (versions, riffs, and imitations inspired by Darío); *trajectory* (following in Darío's footsteps); and *pursuit* (chasing Darío). These meanings converge in "My Rubén," the concluding autobiographical essay. Aragón's beloved poet encompasses his mother's favorite poet—on demand she would recite sentimental lines to young Francisco. And his father's, as well—his favorite Darío poem was the fable of St. Francis of Assisi, reinvented here as "The Man and the Wolf." For Aragón, *my* Rubén is foremost a mariposa poet.

In "Because They Lived Abroad," a Susan Howe epigraph evokes Aragón's method for helping this mariposa poet from his chrysalis: *"to write about a loved author / would be to follow the trails he follows . . ."* On these trails, Aragón's "after" poems tease the limits of "straight" translation. He queers his Darío versions, or finds the queer that's already there. He plays with the poem's body, moving it from one language and form into others. Take "I Pursue a Shape," where Aragón turns Darío's Venus de Milo and Sleeping Beauty into David and "he." How, with these changes, can the "fountain's / spout" and "swan's neck" in the last stanza *not* be read as already queer?

After Rubén imagines durable, graceful forms of belonging, often in the face of exclusion. Many poems borrow and incorporate lines by other poets, creating collective texts across time, space, and languages. If literary property is an illusion, an idea dear to many poets of the Americas, from Borges to Latinx poets such as Urayoán Noel, *my* Rubén doesn't entail ownership. Rather, *my* denotes a tradition to be claimed and fought for, as well as an intimate way of reading and being to be shared—a gift, meal, story, hug, a kind word, a poem.

The penultimate poem, "Poem Beginning with a Fragment of Andrés Montoya," exemplifies this process. The first line, *"the taco vender/reciting/darío/ in a moment/of passion,"* comes from the late Chicano poet from Fresno. Five voices—Montoya, vender, Darío, Aragón, and Leticia Hernández-Linares, to whom the poem is dedicated—become a sensual body. In Austin, where the poem unfolds, we glimpse far-flung Latinx poets "in the open air talking / shop." They share food and words. Such acts of communion constitute Francisco Aragón's contribution to the mariposa tradition. Let's welcome him to his place at the table.

I

2012

24th & Mission BART station laundry
hamper wide screen television Dupont
Circle cassette of my sister's voice cassette
of my father's Court House Metro
torn photograph of my abuelo
"Untitled" by Malaquias Montoya smart
phone theater programs my father's
gold watch boxed up photographs lap-
top Fair Oaks the Mission Noe Valley
skateboard *Mandorla* *The New Yorker*
Venus in Fur *Sex with Strangers* a few
DVDs *Azul* *PALABRA* I was a short
skinny boy *Midnight in Paris* Yuba Poppie
depression *My Vocabulary Did This to Me*

POEM WITH CITATIONS FROM THE O.E.D.

First: *voz* because I recall the taste
of beans wrapped in a corn
tortilla—someone brings it
to me, retrieves what's left
on the plate, the murmured vowels

taking root, taking hold—mi
lengua materna. Then later learn
another spelling, label the "box"
where sound's produced, draw too
the tongue, the teeth, the lips. *The voyce*

that is dysposid to songe and melody
hath thyse proprytees: smalle,
subtyll, thicke, clere, sharpe . . .
in 1398. But what
of the deaf-mute, his winning shout

—BINGO!—knocking me over?
Huxley noted: *voice may exist*
without speech and speech may exist
without voice. The first time I spoke
with my father was on the phone, so his

was all I had to go on: that,
and what he'd say—things he'd hear
"inside." In *Doctor's Dilemma*
Shaw wrote: *When my patients*
tell me they hear voices

I lock them up. The pitch, the tone, the range:
a way of trying to know him. Now hers
and his are in the pages of a book:
Un baile de máscaras by Sergio
Ramírez, his characters echoing

words, rhythms I heard
until she died, hearing them as well
for months after whenever I spoke
with him. *Who hath not shared that calm*
so still and deep, The voiceless thought

which would not speak but weep

POSTCARD

Blue sky the Bay
Bridge from afar
arcing like a bow

to Treasure Island
—city skyline
scoring a view

tourists could buy
at Fisherman's Wharf
but for the smudge

clouding the tip
of the Pyramid; panels
deflecting the sun

glint through, as if a beacon
shrouded in fog
were blinking a code

to this green slope: park
named after a mission:
Dolores   Dolores

—it simmers on my tongue, is
Pains in Spanish, is
her name. And beyond the grass

a dark-haired woman
crouching in the sand
saying to a boy

¡Sácate los dedos
de la boca!
Take your fingers

out of your mouth!

Reasons Why She Didn't

stay. Pavement
was one. And doors—

a front door
beyond which

24th & Mission
blared. The preacher

at the BART
station's concrete

lip seemed odd
to her—the way

most mornings he
was pretty much

ignored. Mamá
is arm in arm

with her: a walk
she'll take

on her own in
Tipitapa

FAR AWAY

(*Rubén Darío*)

Ox I saw
as a child, breath
little clouds
of steam, vivid

in the sun, Nicaragua
a fertile ranch
abundant, rhythms
tropic, dove in a forest

of sound—wind,
bird, bull, ax:
the core
of me are these

and these I praise
yes, ox: lumbering
you evoke tender
dawn, the milking hour

when days were white
and rose, and you
cooing mountain
dove recall

April   May
when spring
was all was
everything

JUGGLERS

She and I on a bench peeling prawns:

the first day of her fiftieth year and she points
at street performers about to juggle
fire, and a distant summer morning

surfaces, afloat on the light wind blowing
off the bay—older sisters in the dark, hiding
as big brother parades around the house

his hands outstretched clutching large candles
I'm on a search! he shouts,
marching from room to room

till he finds them huddling in a jungle
of clothes, beacons flickering as flame-
hot wax begins to flow across his fingers

while she is walking to Centro Adulto, her head brimming
with phrases: the words she needs so she can quit
sewing, land a job in a bank . . . and the sitter

arriving minutes late, finding us wet
and trying to save a coat, a shirt, a dress—it's
a small one: nothing the green hose

and frantic assembly-line of buckets
doesn't eventually douse, leaving walls and curtains
the color of coal—¡Mira! she gasps

her left hand rapping my shoulder, still pointing with the right
as the torches,
from one juggler to the other,

begin to fly

for my mother (1932–1997)

Photo, 1945

The only photo of you, black and white
and torn—the frayed edge
climbing your chest, just missing

your left eye, cutting
off your ear: only your face
was spared. The link

is your daughter, youngest
of eleven. Lifting
the hem of her cotton dress

above her knees, she lowers herself
onto pebbles and beans
you've carefully arranged

on the ground. Sitting nearby
you raise your head, peering
over the pages of *La Prensa*

to discipline a child with your eyes:
until you think she's had enough,
she kneels perfectly still.

Later, you rise from your chair
and stretch, noting in the distance
a slice of sun, how it hovers

over Momotombo, smearing fire
across a jagged horizon:
time for drinks and a game

of cards, when a certain mood
seeps into your skin—hurry, they're waiting
for you to deal the first hand.

Summer air laced with insect
sounds soon fills
with the small bells of Pedro's

approaching cart, peddling the ice
he scrapes and then flavors
with syrup. Knowing you well, she

scrambles to the table,
your chair, but you're ahead of her:
having heard the jingling too,

you've set aside a few *córdobas*
next to your tin cup of beer.
Your large dark hand cups

the back of my mother's head
as you kiss her forehead
in front of your friends, pressing

the coins into her palm. Abuelo,
I'm holding you
in my fingers—a broken window

you gaze from, a face
I've never really seen,
or touched.

FOTO, 1945

La única foto de ti, en blanco y negro
y rota—el borde desgastado
escalando tu pecho, rozando

tu ojo izquierdo, cortando
tu oreja: sólo tu cara
se salvó. El lazo

es tu hija, la más joven
de once. Subiéndose
el vestido de algodón

por encima de las rodillas, dobla
sus piernas sobre los guijarros y frijoles
que con cuidado has

esparcido en la tierra. Sentado cerca
levantas la cabeza, asomándote
por encima de *La Prensa*

para disciplinar a una niña con tu mirada:
hasta que creas que ha sido suficiente
se queda arodillada sin moverse.

Luego, te levantas de tu silla
y te estiras, notando en la distancia
una tajada de sol, y cómo se cierne

sobre Momotombo, untando fuego
a lo largo del horizonte montañoso:
hora de echarse unos tragos

y una partida, cuando un cierto humor
se mete bajo tu piel. Apúrate,
esperan que repartas las cartas.

Aire veraniego se mezcla con sonidos
de insectos, llenándose pronto
con las campanillas del carrito

de Pedro, que se acerca con su hielo
para raspar y añadir sabor
de frutas. Conociéndote bien, ella

corre hacia la mesa
a tu silla, pero te le has adelantado:
habiendo oído también el tintineo

has apartado unos cuantos córdobas
junto a tu tarro de cerveza.
Tu gran mano moreno sujeta por detrás

la cabeza de mi madre
al besarle la frente
delante de tus amigos, apretando

las monedas en su palma. Abuelo,
te tengo
entre mis dedos—una ventana

rota por la que atisbas: una cara
que nunca he visto
de verdad, ni he tocado.

GLORIA'S

In the photograph, my father has his back to the camera. He's leaning forward reaching down, about to lift a shuttered metal security door. His dress shirt is slightly untucked, the sleeves bunched at the elbow. *Gloria's*, a second-hand clothing store, is named after his second wife, who was born in El Salvador.

It's my sister Maria's freshman year at Immaculate Conception Academy. After school, she hops on the 14 and rides to the Outer Mission in San Francisco to shop at the store. She usually picks out one item—a scarf, a belt, a blouse. When she tries handing my father her dollar bills, he waves them away. For her, it's an excuse to visit him two, three times a month. Conceived in Nicaragua, Maria is my father's firstborn. She was ten when he left.

After our mother's funeral decades later, my siblings and I share family stories and Maria says that Gloria often seemed sad—the blank expression on her face hiding something, perhaps. Gloria often wore large dark glasses.

Some days, Maria takes us along and all four of us visit our father. I walk down a corridor of bins that are as tall as I am, brimming with "the bargains," as opposed to the slacks and sweaters and dresses that hang from racks. The word "Gloria's" is thickly printed on blue wooden paneling above the doorway outside, a rainbow brightly depicted beside it. One afternoon, Gloria is holding in her arms an infant with black unruly hair.

And then there's this: a short wrinkled woman, unmoving, just visible in the back. Whether she's sitting or standing I can't tell. Someone whispers her name is Juana. Someone whispers she's Dad's mom. I have no memory of her speaking. Maria, on the other hand, does: on a day Gloria isn't in the store, on a day my father is busy on the phone, Maria, tentative, approaches her and says, Hola. The wrinkled woman speaks:

Why do you keep coming here? Can't you see he has a new family? There's no need for you or the others to drop by. I know what you're up to. ¡Vete! And don't come back.

My father replaces the receiver and sees Maria lift her hand to her mouth, swivel, and swiftly head for the door. "What's wrong," he calls out, in pursuit. "¿Qué te pasa?" as he catches up and holds her by the arm. Maria, without looking up, tells him, her voice unsteady. "Ay don't pay any attention to her," he sneers. "¡Es una vieja loca!"

ERNESTO CARDENAL IN BERKELEY

1982

The books in my backpack
felt lighter walking
down the stairs at 24th & Mission. The sky
was clear and I wasn't heading for school . . .

Above, at the station's mouth, a preacher
wove Spanish while beyond him
on the ground a whiskered man
snored through the morning, his trousers

soiled. A thought flickered, swayed
(*Rubén Darío in Madrid* . . .) as I rode
east along the floor
of the bay; commuters dozed,

later did crosswords going home, more
of them boarding at Embarcadero,
Montgomery, Powell. After
the reading I was a notebook

filled—mamá y papá juntos a different
life billowing inside me:
a dusty street in Granada
or León, playing baseball;

or picturing in class how
Francisco Hernández de Córdoba
is led across the plaza he himself
had traced out with his sword,

beheaded

BLISTER

the noun

A disease
of the peach tree
—a fungus

distorts leaves.
The first time
I was taken

to see him
I was five
or six. A vesicle

on the skin
containing
serum, caused

by friction,
a burn, or other
injury. He lived

on Alabama Street
near Saint
Peter's and wore

a white T-shirt,
starched and snug.
A similar swelling

with fluid
or air
on the surface

of a plant,
or metal
after cooling

or the sunless
area between
one's toes

after a very
long walk.
Don't ask me

how it is I
ended up
holding it.

An outer
covering
fitted to a

vessel to protect
against torpedos,
mines, or to improve

stability. My guess
is that he
brought it out

to show me
thinking, perhaps,
I had never

seen one
up close,
let alone felt

the blunt weight
of one
in my hands.

A rounded
compartment
protruding

from the body
of a plane.
What came

next: no
image but
sensation of

its hammer
(my inexpert
manipulation)

digging
into but not
breaking

skin—the spot
at the base
of my thumb

balloons,
filling slowly
with fluid . . .

In Spanish:
ampolla
—*an Ampul*

of chrystal
in the Middle
Ages could be

a relic containing
the blood
of someone

holy. I'm fairly
certain it wasn't
loaded.

CALLE MOMOTOMBO

Managua, the '50s

I

Nights, I step
in, take a seat
beside her

sewing machine,
stay until one,
two, platicando—

cómo me encanta
la madrugada.
Months leading

up to Christmas
blur, filling
orders—vestidos,

camisas, skirts. We
leave the door
open and greet

who strolls up,
down the street. Nada
de peligro,

safe

II

They're tending el puesto
Yolanda, Sandra, Conchita . . .
And since I'm Lolita's
novio, I say, ¿Dónde

está? She's inside
doing the dishes
—all I need to know:
como un gato I tiptoe

towards her, the faucet
more spring than
faucet, the incessant
sound of water

masking my steps—
soft, soft from behind
until I raise both
hands and curl

my arms firmly
around, cover
her eyes, envuelto
en mis brazos,

her back up
against my chest
—tight. Of course
she knows: no one

touches her
like this. This
is a dream—well,
not that exactly, but

a message, spirit
to spirit—this scene
nothing she's
ever recalled

in person

II

Keough Hall

November 9, 2016
University of Notre Dame

"deplorables
knocking
at your door"

he shouted
the day
after—"build

the wall—
we're
building

a wall
around
your room!"

minutes
felt
like hours

"cowards!"
you managed,
catching

a glimpse
by cracking
your door:

there were three
of them
scurrying

down the hall,
their faces
obscured . . .

your back
against
the wall, you slid

to the floor—
"Hail Mary . . ."
you began

whispering
to yourself
and back

they came their
laughter
louder

minutes
felt
like hours

and the thumping
in your chest—
his fist

pounding the door

for Gregory Jenn ('18)

The Inevitable

I envy that tree.
It barely feels.
Envy even more
this stone
that hasn't felt
for ages. Tell me
of an affliction
more acute
than breathing,
of something worse
than knowing
that we are, yet
knowing nothing,
unsure of which
path to take.
And what to make
of this sense
we're on a wheel,
uncanny hunch
of bleaker things
to come, the only truth
one day we die?
We endure this life,
shadows, what we
ignore and hardly
suspect, skin that glows
like a shimmering piece
of fruit, visions
of a wreath
beside a tomb, all
the while without
a clue

of where we began,
where we go.

after Rubén Darío's "Lo fatal"

To George W. Bush

2006

Should I quote the good
book you claim to know;

or perhaps our late bearded
bard—might these be ways

of reaching you? Primitive
modern, simple complex—

one part wily astute
animal, three parts owner

of a ranch: conglomeration
is what you are, poised

for another incursion.
Lean, strong specimen

of your breed, polite you
hardly read when not

in a saddle, or spreading manure.
You see a building in flames

as vital, progress a spewing
volcano. And where you point

and place your bullet
you stake the future—yours

and ours. And so:
not so fast. O there's

no doubting the heft
of this nation: it moves it

shifts—a tremor travels
down to the tip

of the continent; you raise
your voice and it's

bellowing we hear (*The sky
is mine*), stars in the east

sun in the west. People
are clothes, their cars,

Sunday attire at church,
a harbor lady lighting

the journey with a torch.
But America, sir,

is North, Central,
and South—delicate

wing of a beetle,
thundering sheet

of water (our cubs
are crossing

over). And though,
O man of bluest eye

you believe your truth,
it is not—*you* are not

the world

after Rubén Darío's "A Roosevelt"

TENOCHTITLAN, 1523

strange   while fishing
sun   lowering itself
everyone wondered
                    unknown bird   the vision
            over and over
            men   rode
throwing
        blades
            a new game   men
wild   with
    hunting
chopped   skin
                        burnt feet
            all of it
stench
                                            pain
                                    the
surprise   shock   so
so   so
    desire   everything
not enough.

an erasaure of Andrés Montoya

Wind & Rain

And that day years ago—no
umbrella, the stroll
lasting four hours, your socks

soaked—*doesn't matter*
you thought: crossing, re-crossing
the Thames on foot sheer

pleasure, coming upon
Leicester Square, that throng . . .
—*What happened?*

to a petite lady wearing glasses, but
before she could speak
a slick wall of coats

slowly parts and there
he was: plum-colored,
rolling past on a stretcher . . .

Moments later they cover his face.
The rest of your walk
a blur . . . —*I think his heart*

gave, said a man wearing
a tie, but those weren't the ones
that spoke to you, still do:

poor chap, softly, her light-blue
hair in your eyes . . . *and his wife.*
I saw the ring. expecting him home

for supper

1985

Long and black, the streaks
of gray, aflutter in the light
wind as she prepares to tell

her story at the Federal Building:
reaching into a tattered sack
she pulls out a doll

missing an eye, balding—
singed face smudged with soot
from the smoke her home took in

as her village was being shelled.
Next she retrieves what's left
of a book—a few pages

the borders brown, coming
apart in her hands: hesitant,
she raises one, starts to read aloud:

por la mañana sube el sol y calienta el día
la tierra nos da dónde vivir y qué comer
la vaca nos da leche para beber y hacer mantequilla

It's her daughter's lesson
the poem she read to her
the day they struck—

(in the morning the sun rises and warms the day
the earth provides a place to live and what to eat
the cow gives us milk to drink and churn butter with . . .)

. . . mid-way through, her voice begins
to shake—her words
like refugees exposed to the night shiver,

freeze: silence
swallows us all . . .
. . . her words, drifting

casualities,
gather and huddle
in my throat.

San Francisco

POEM WITH A PHRASE OF ISHERWOOD

2010, Arizona

Cruelty is sensual and stirs you
Governor, your name echoing the sludge
beneath your cities' streets. It spurs

the pleasure you take
whenever your mouth nears
a mic, defending your law . . . your wall.

Cruelty is sensual and stirs you
Governor, we've noticed your face
its contortions and delicate sneer

times you're asked to cut
certain ribbons—visit a dusty place
you'd rather avoid, out of the heat.

Cruelty is sensual and stirs you
Governor, the vision of your state
something you treasure in secret

though we've caught a glimpse
in the jowls of your sheriff:
bulldog who doubles as your heart.

BAY AREA RAPID TRANSIT

Her hair: cropped short as a punk's, same
gray as these connected cars; her pullover's blue
snug, the few holes along her sleeves

flesh-colored sores. She's cursing the crooks
at City Hall—*then go back to where you are from*
he says, off in a huff at Powell. On her feet now

she spots another facing the light-streaked black,
crosses the aisle, sits beside him. The puffy skin
beneath her eyes: pinkish—*I hate this place*, she says

holding an envelope in his face—*could you
help me with this address they cut
me off those boys what they did to that girl*

outside my room on the stairs . . . And the joints
of her fingers: bulbs—*I was you know
a typist in New York . . . O,* she says, *what'll I*

*do do you know this address what should I
tell them I swear sometimes
if maybe I just*—her voice dissolving,

mingling with the long sharp whistle
the sound of the rails as the convoy
begins to brake and then the sliding

doors and steps off the train

DECEMBER 31, 1965

The hoped-for words went out
And so, as dusk settled over the embattled
Not since the first winter of World War I
The idea of a holiday from death
As if in anticipation of the lull
Throughout the world, hopes rose
Pope Paul VI exhorted
President Johnson steadfastly refused
"They are outsiders, just as I am," snapped Truman
The foursome, accused of burning their cards
The Army meanwhile made clear that dissent was for civilians
Howe was sentenced to two years
In the bitter Harlem riots of 1964, as in the Watts
Last week, under a 1901 New York law
Epton was no ordinary agitator
Long before the riots, according to a Negro detective who infiltrated the group
As he made the rounds of Jersey City's sprawling Medical
"If there is a toe in town I haven't stepped on
"City jobs around here were just plain patronage plums
"A man doesn't carry that much fat around and live
Wrapped perennially in a white linen suit
At one celebrated Boykinalia
There was salmon from Quebec
The voters' love for Boykin ran out in the 1962
He is now 80 and after all those lovin' years has an ailing heart
A year before he was arrested for the nightrider slaying
Klansman Collie Leroy Wilkins was riding around with a sawed-off
Judge Allgood last week sentenced Wilkins to a year and a day

TIME *Magazine*

The Man and the Wolf

His heart the texture of a rose,
his tongue a swath of sky,
his manner delicate—now

chatting with what many call
a beast: the look in the eyes rabid,
black: on the skirts of the village

devoured sheep and shepherd alike.
Men skilled with iron were routed.
Fangs shredded hunting dogs

like baby lamb. So out he went
looking for his den, found him
outside it, from where the animal

lunged at the sight of him, then saw
the hand rise, heard him say:
"Peace be with you, brother wolf."

The mammal knew that gesture,
snapped out of it and froze:
"Oh, it's you." "Why,"

asked the man, "must you lead
this life? The blood your snout
spills; the grief and terror

you mete out; peasants sobbing,
who are children of God . . .
Does this please you? Are you

from hell, or perhaps consumed
by some eternal ire?" And the wolf,
subdued, said: "Winter is hard

"and hunger worse in a freezing
forest that yields nothing to eat.
It's true: I looked for livestock

"to feed on, and did, and ate
shepherds too. As for blood,
the hunter on his horse gripping

"his metal pursuing boar, bear,
and deer—sheds more. I've seen scores
of them inflict wounds, torture

"God's creatures. And hunger
is not what drives *them* to hunt."
To which the man responded: "Evil

exists in humans. We are born
with sin. But the simple soul of a beast
is pure. From this day on you'll have

enough to eat. And you will leave
the people of this land, and their flocks,
alone. May God appease that side

of you." "Okay, it's a deal."
"As a gesture of faith extend
your paw—let's shake on it."

The wolf did as asked and lifted
his foot. The man wrapped his
fingers around it, gently squeezed.

They headed for the village. People
could hardly believe their eyes: the wolf
strode behind the man in the robe

like a family dog, his head bowed.
Every man, woman, and child
came closer, until the whole village

had gathered in the plaza where
the man began to speak: "Let me
introduce a new neighbor," he said,

pointing to the wolf with an open
hand. "Fear him not. He is
our enemy no more. In return,

I'm going to ask that each of us
do our part and feed him. He is,
after all, a creature of God."

The village responded as one:
"So be it!" The wolf raised
his head in acknowledgement,

moving his tail from side to side,
disappeared through the gates
of a convent, the man ahead of him.

For a time the wolf was at peace
in that place. His ears would fill
with psalms—his eyes with tears.

He learned how to move with grace,
to play pranks in the kitchen.
When the man whispered his prayers,

the wolf would pass his tongue across
his sandals. Out into the street
he'd go, through the valley, over hills,

into homes, where people gave him things
to eat. To them he seemed a docile hound.
And then the man had to leave

for a time. The sweet wolf, the good
and gentle wolf vanished and went
back into the hills. The howling began

again. Once more people were filled
with fear, villages nearby with dread.
Weapons and valor were useless, the rage

never letting up, as if something
burned, smoldered inside the beast.
The day the man returned, villagers

sought him out, wept their complaints
about the suffering inflicted—that
infamous creature was at it again.

A shadow passed over the man's face.
He headed for the hills to track
him down—that butcher of a wolf.

He found him at his cave. "In the name
of the Father, who sees it all, what
have you got to say for yourself?!"

As if in pain, the animal spoke,
his mouth foaming, his eyes nearly
swollen shut. "Don't come any closer . . .

Peace and calm were my masters
these days. Even with you gone
I visited the village. When given

scraps to eat, I chewed, swallowed
in silence, with gratitude.
But I began to see, in many homes,

how people treat each other,
embers of greed, intolerance, lies
glowing subtly in countless faces.

The weak were losers, the cruel winners.
Brother made war on brother. Male
and female were like dog and bitch,

and then they began to beat me,
considered me weak for licking
their hands and feet. I believed

you: all of creation were family—
men my siblings, oxen too, the stars
my sisters, my brothers worms.

But they picked on me, drove
me away. Their laughing was like
scalding water, re-awakening

a beast—suddenly a 'bad' wolf
is what I was, yet better than most
of them. And so the struggle

to survive took over: to defend myself,
to feed myself, like the bear does,
like the boar, who, in order to live,

must kill. So let me remain here,
wild and free. And you, my friend,
back to your people, your good

and tender deeds." The man
didn't say a word. Deep
was his gaze. Then he walked away,

tears on his cheek. His heart,
touched with desolation, offered
a prayer only the wind in the forest

could hear, carrying it skyward.

after Rubén Darío's "Los motivos del lobo"

Liu Minghe Speaks

A hyena upon an animal still breathing, he questioned me
I was told it would last for days
His voice clutched my frozen heart
My lungs burned my temples throbbed—night revolving my eyes
A silent tribe of spiders began spinning a web in my brain
Bells occasionally howled—homeless spirits endlessly moaning
I was handcuffed to a window, so I stood, or hung, from my wrists
Several of my lower teeth left me during my visit
To open, with a withered hand, the lid of a coffin, and climb inside

At first, I didn't butter my hair
I breakfasted on air, on rock, on coal, on iron
My clothes were rotting rags, my bread soggy with rain
I ate by lowering my head into a bowl
I ate fever with my watery vegetables
For sixteen months my hands and feet were shackled
I slept on boards, or on the ground—a book
Les Poètes Maudits my pillow, my only companion
My skin was ravaged with mud, my armpits full of worms

Enormous province whose sky is flecked with fire and mud
Weighing on me like a lid
Pouring down days as dark as nights
Sometimes the rain mimicked the bars
Funeral processions—no drums, no music—filed slowly inside me
Hope wept, stabbing its stalk in my skull
Sometimes I saw in the sky endless beaches
I tried to invent new flowers, new tongues, new stars
Fear and suffering evaporating in the air
The hallucination of words

On my hospital bed that smell comes back to me still
I have dyed my hair black to erase those years

Helen Speaks

June, 2017

Tonight I will sit in the dark
people the wall of my sorrow

Roberto was a busser I was a server
he came to visit an aunt and stayed

he started talking and I tried
to ignore him he kept on talking

smiling and smiling and smiling
full of smiles and careful words

we got married had three kids
settled into a comfortable life

I wanted to understand the madness
the sad slouch of justice

we met in '98 in Fort Wayne
years and years went by until

Eddie's Steak Shed in Granger
we lived in Mishawaka

your husband is being detained
because he's a fugitive they said

my husband's not running
from you you didn't come

knocking on our door I said
he came to you he'd been told

to leave in 2000 I was pregnant
and sick and so again he stayed

he's been moved from Wisconsin
to Lousiana and more recently

El Paso Texas one night they
suddenly told him it was time

to get his stuff put him in the back
of a van sped for the border

he was dropped off forced
to walk to Mexico the children

eight-year-old Demetri fourteen-year-old
Jasmine sixteen-year-old Maria

are having a difficult time
since he's been gone the restaurant

has received threatening calls
and angry letters pack your bags

and go to Mexico said one
earlier today staring in the mirror:

your skin is bitter like suffering
what have you done voting for trump

with Andrés Montoya

ACADEMIA ESCOLAR

Managua, the '40s

Her look
could undo. Not

the most soothing thing I could say . . .
The day they said we'd

be let out early
a bubbly mood spread

among us as we planned
the afternoon—impromptu

stick ball, that dusty lot . . .
The Academy's front gate

clicked
shut behind us

when someone saw her
behind a car, arms

folded across her chest.
I had no reason to, but

that unexpected sight
made me flinch—

an eight-year-old child
frightened. Think

about it. A boy.
Afraid of his mother.

for my father

The Century

Episode two with Peter Jennings
—Adolph, as a young man,
was denied entry to Art School.
What could be worse than a bitter

mediocre artist with a plan?
In the second segment you see
a physicist at twenty-four, the moving
picture a grainy gray—he nibbles

a strawberry, sips a flute of cava, swings
in his moments of free time
a racket, his stint at Los Alamos
intense. The Manhattan Project.

Today another face—captured,
bruised—on *Good Morning America*:
the screen says *Lopez* and I see a trace
of him: my brother at seventeen,

those postcards home from Camp
Pendleton, the scribbled pride
of his "ass-kicking platoon." Reading
them I was following him: ten-year-old

as future marine—like chanting
oblivious, the rich syllables
of a word, a slogan
a country, that man's name.

1999

III

PORTRAIT WITH LINES OF MONTALE

A patch of town-sick country

The old shop window shuttered and harmless
An odor of bruised melons oozes from the floor
Among wicker furniture and a mattress

Mildew like grass sprouts as well
The delicate capillaries of slime
Signs of quite another orbit

The ungraspable gorge
Sentiments and sediment
Where my carved name quivers

His laugh is jagged coughing

for my father

We Talk Dogs

Or the one Maria found, trotting
along the banks of the Yuba—
the river his name, red

scarf around the snowy neck
that week of camping, coaxed
onto the backseat and taken home . . .

He mentions one—de raza alemana, he says
and I'm almost charmed by the voice:
telling how he'd tie his German

shepherd to a pole, escort her
to church: Plaza Santo
Domingo flanked by the park, kiosk

beside the roasting beef, pleasant
olor de carne asada wafting
to the bench after mass

where they talked—she mostly:
her sewing, her trip to Panama
in search of wholesale fabrics . . .

—I'm trying to picture it: Managua
in the fifties, my father's
plane lifting off, touching

down, sending for her months later,
big with Maria, as I'm also
trying to picture him

on the other end of the line: in his
sixties, portly, sugar
in his blood, a whiff of something

on his breath as he speaks
of the Sacramento
River: pole and gear, sixpack,

Rocky and Comet slinking behind
—*but the car's busted now*, he says
basting in gravel

near Chico. He gets to bed
past three, watching *Cristina,*
the Tuesday Night Fights, sunk

in a beat-up armchair:
replay of that memorable bout, Aaron
Pryor delivering a blur of shots

to the head, Alexis Arguello absorbing them . . .
During the phone call
we talk dogs. He had three,

we had two—something
I suppose, in common;
this talk of ours

a first.

VOICES

In bed, yes, during a state
between sleep and wakefulness:
she'd speak to me then, spirit

to spirit—not speech, exactly,
but a voice from her realm
to mine, though once she sang

"Caminito" by Carlos Gardel.

A large picture of me
in a white T-shirt taken
by a photographer friend.

She had it framed, placed
atop the dresser. "What became
of it?" I whispered to her . . .

I stuffed it in the drawer.
Didn't feel like looking
at you anymore.

Once, she talked about my shirts,
the ones I did the plumbing in.

She'd put them on the pillow
to trick herself, closing her eyes:

I still slept, still snored beside her.

I cursed, swore, spit a palabrota
and off she bolted. Playa Pochomil.
Have you seen her, I said, and friends

pointed to the trucks, so I scoured
the beach, looking and looking

till finally I spotted her, crouched
up on a bluff overlooking

the surf. *I saw you*, she whispered,
calling my name.
I was testing you.

While in bed, yes, during a state
between sleep and wakefulness:
she'd speak to me then, spirit

to spirit—not speech, exactly,
but a voice from her realm
to mine, though once she sang

"Caminito" by Carlos Gardel.

NICARAGUA IN A VOICE

More than the poems
—the fruits that sang
their juices; dolls, feverish,
dreaming of nights,

city streets—for me it was
the idle chat *between* the poems:
cordial, intimate almost . . .
like a river's murmur

as if a place—León,
Granada—could speak,
whistle, inhabit
a timbre . . . as if, closing

my eyes, I had it again,
once more within reach:
his voice—my father
unwell, won't speak.

Canción

A dog I love growls
at the sight of me,

can no longer bear
his diablos, crazed

with the *here, there,*
how, all around him

the air howling. I sense
temptation to dive

into the void—glint
of his coat, hint

of a yelp a blade
to the throat.

Unclench, I say;
look: your ghost

father swims
in your ghost mother,

opens his snout
in your direction,

the sound reaching you,
soothes your sleep,

puts out the blaze
in your head,

is a quilt wrapped
around you, unfurls

down the path you tread,
or flaps in the wind

while you feed, keeps
you company, though

your spirit
is still a fuse—

Seashell

(Rubén Darío)

Half-hidden in the sand
is where I find it—embroidered
with golden pearls like the one
she held, riding over the water

on a bull. To my lips
I raise it, provoke echoes . . .
then press it to my ear
to hear the bluest fathoms

whisper of their riches.
This is how the salt
of a storm slowly fills me,
how those sails billowed

when stars fell for Jason.
And I listen to the voice
of a wave—deep
indecipherable wind . . . (the shell

is in the shape of a heart)

for Antonio Machado

After Fragments of Juan Felipe Herrera

Hands:

Small, brown, like your father's, cradle the timepiece he gave you, your eyes
looking down at it, your feet half in, half out, the Pacific, your shorts cut-
offs, frayed, your T-shirt white, like the one he wears in the photograph,
Marlon Brando in *A Streetcar Named Desire*, you half laugh a little, lips
slightly parted, if only you could talk into the wee hours, that time you vis-
ited twenty years ago, instead you mumble to yourself, your legs fatigued,
blemished, you hadn't noticed, phantom days, phantom nights, and now
pretending to run along this shore, esta orilla, you have arrived by chance,
re-creating him—in this poem

Eyes:

Here I am again, attempting to swim, my breast stroke reduced to rubble
after decades of sifting, the years, I hadn't noticed how flabby my arms had
become, giggling in the moonlight a distant memory, summer nights we
sneaked out, down to that corner of the river no one spoke of openly, side
by side we would laugh and lick, laugh and lick, giving new meaning to a
phrase, *slip of the tongue*, and no buttons to undo, no shirts to strain to see
through, the rags of our clothes in a heap back at the cabin, instead the wet
sand films our arms, our hands, our legs, as we cross, easily, the sea of our
gaze

A WAVE

of the past as I walk
by a window boarded-up

breaks—cold
in winter and in

summer hot where
spiders lived and dust

filmed everything
in that storefront

that was his home. Or
a madcap air in May

or a combination
of words can bring

a voice to the surface
—it's that I . . . at the

thought of him
which, more today

than yesterday,
is like approaching

a grave. His calls
before my first visit

flickered weekly,
are ash now. Cities

changed their names:
Madrid became

Corning became Davis,
South Bend,

D.C. I know
the beginnings

and the ends
of things. I

curb myself,
swallow what

cannot change.
But still, it is

there (he who
was torn

away no
longer

needs). But isn't
it time this grew

fruitful, time
I loose myself

and, though unsteady,
move on—the way

the arrow, suddenly
all vector

survives the string?

with Akhmatova and Rilke
for my father

HOTEL MIRROR

Looking I thought: *hair.*
And a voice said
On your head? where?

Who is that staring back
with such a round face,
that paunch? Father

or son?

IV

WALT

His country of iron where he lives: an older man, fatherly,
     strong, wholesome, calm,
his appearance impressive—the furrow of his brow
     persuades and charms, no end

to his soul that mimics a mirror, the tired curve of
     his shoulders draped with a cloak;
and with his harp—carved from oak—he sings his song
     like a prophet. He's a priest

fueling a wind that promises and promises . . . *Fly!* he says
     to an eagle, to a seaman: *Row!*
while a chiseled, robust worker hears: *Put your shoulder*
     to the wheel! This is the path

our poet takes
—magnificent

face

    after Rubén Darío's "Walt Whitman"

Because They Lived Abroad

to write about a loved author
would be to follow the trails he follows . . .
—Susan Howe

—or Rubén's Parisian phase
How during those nine
months he and Amado
shared an apartment
in Montmartre
rue du Faubourg
their all-consuming flesh
their melancholy exile
Stood where Vallejo would
the melancholia of Darío
Nervo Vallejo   Between them
shared what they lacked
We track our own desire
that *soul-is-content* paradox
as in those lines that still
pulsing beneath the skin
y no saber adonde vamos
ni de donde venimos

————

Because they lived abroad
I was away for years
What meaning is there
in my head   these names
Free as oceans bottles
are what they are
another kind of mirror
material for a start
Consider all of this
an excursus on origins

trace of the word *lugar*
I will inhabit a place
that doesn't exist
Hay golpes en la vida
tan fuertes . . . Yo no sé
Managua is Madrid

To the Old World

Days I walked around swathes of you
Whose names slip my mind
I'm thirsty—come to me flowing
Down my throat: billboards posters
Doorplates twittering like parakeets
Through heaven came flying a thousand pigeons
I strode alone through your crowds
Buses in herds rolling by
I stood at the counters of your dirty bars
I ate in your restaurants at night
Often at long tables sharing a bottle of wine
Most mornings a milkman
Clinked glass along a lane
In the perpetual screeching of wheels
I heard a song
And my ears like taillights trail behind to hear it still
The great hearth of you with the intersecting
Embers of your streets—your old buildings
Leaning over them for warmth
And beneath: I rubbed elbows with your shuddering Metros
Some of them bellowing like bulls
The cry of their whistles could tear me apart
The skies above your plazas
Would turn deepening shades of violet
And your waves of traffic footsteps and the smell already
Of chestnuts roasting in a barrel on a corner
Your parks were lungs
Your air crisp enough to taste sprinkled
With sputtering Vespas and horns
Your newly scrubbed
Neoclassic façades I loved looking at
And faces—faces glanced or gazed at
Waiting for lights to change

Once   not sidewalks but   one   wide   walk—
Cars streaming up and down both sides of it
With merchant pavilions on my right and left:
Newsagents florists pet sellers and their chirping cages
Or descending stairs for a stroll behind a clear blue
Thundering sheet of water
And let me remember well the white-haired man
Descending ahead of us
Off the plane
How something in me fluttered hearing his vowels
Hearing in the sound of his voice
A message I'd take years to unravel as I venture
To inhabit once again your cities my self

with Apollinaire and Cendrars

I Pursue a Shape

I pursue
          a shape

which
to my style remains
elusive

     bud
   of a thought
that wants to unfurl

that arrives
with a kiss
alighting

on my lips
like being hugged
by David

columns
are adorned
with palms

stars say
I will glimpse
a god

and light
descends
settling

inside me
like the bird
of the moon

settling
on a still lake
and yet all

I obtain are
words wanting
to scurry away

melodious
prelude
streaming

from a flute
boat
of dreams

rowing
through space
and outside

his window
the fountain's
spout continues

to weep
the swan's neck
posing the question

after Rubén Darío's "Yo persigo una forma"

SYMPHONY IN GRAY

(Rubén Darío)

Like glass

the color of mercury
it mirrors the sky's
sheet of zinc, the pale gray
a burnish splotched

with a flock of birds
while the sun's disc
like something injured crawls
slowly to the top

and the wind that blows
off the swells
dozes
in a trough,

its bugle a pillow.
Leaden waves crest
collapse—seeming
to groan near the docks

where he sits on thick
suspended rope,
smokes a pipe, his mind
sifting the sand in a faraway place.

An old wolf is what
he is. The light in Brazil
toasted his face. A strapping
storm from China

saw him tilt a flask of gin.
And foams laced
with salt, iodine
recall his curls, scorched

nose, his biceps
like those of an athlete,
his seaman's cap
and blouse. A screen

of tobacco smoke
lifts as did the fog
off the coast
that blazing noon

he set sail. Siesta
in the tropics. Our wolf
is nodding off—a gray
filming it all, as if the line

denoting the horizon
in a charcoal sketch
were to blur,
disappear. Siesta

in the tropics. Old cicada
is plucking its hoarse
forgetful guitar
while cricket draws

its bow across the one
string on its fiddle.

1916

León, Nicaragua

One evening water—
watching

it fall, the night sweet
silver

the breathing sigh
a sob

the sky's amethyst
soft—

diluting his tears;
the fountain

mingles with
his fate—

song of my own
cascade

after Rubén Darío's "Triste, muy tristemente"

VOICES

A scrap, a phrase
that stretch of pavement
I'd phone him from, sweating

past Saint Matthew's
coming from the Y
along Rhode Island

sun on my face never
his face seen
or touched—now more

than ever: his son-
in-law at the keyboard
not him, answering

the instant message
*I'm afraid I
have bad news . . .*

The night
we sat or knelt
around her

was something I never . . .
Brother driving all
day part of the night

to join us bedside.
(What was it like,
Ron—your heart

giving out?)
The sky
darkens, the drip

of morphine not
enough, the sound
issuing from her

hard to place—
substitute
for breath:

the interval
between each
lengthens . . .

What were some
of the stories?
The first one

you recounted
that day I can't
be sure. Was it

about the time
you toked
up? The warm

breeze
a comfort, you said
as I started

the cassette.
Where does it
begin, this need

to preserve?
Yours was strong
and sure, easy

to listen to, not
what one
might expect—

sturdy as the metal
table and chairs
in the patio

we lounged on.
Driving you
to Sebastopol

for treatments.
Learning the route
by heart. That July

on leave, I swooned
in ways I hadn't
those years

you lived north
of us—San
Rafael, Sonoma,

Santa Rosa,
Petaluma . . .
Was recording

you a way of
releasing you?
The months

you lived
as a child
among cousins

in Managua
who didn't
know a word

of English
your voice
was a bridge.

Is a voice
on a tape
a bridge?

Sounds
the living
make,

the dying,
the dead.

for Maria Aragon (1956–2004)

In November of 2012, Arizona State University issued a press release announcing the acquisition of a privately-held collection of manuscripts created by Nicaraguan poet Rubén Darío. The collection consists of 900 or so handwritten pages of poetry, essays, stories, and personal letters, nine of which revealed for the first time an intimate relationship between Darío and famed Mexican poet Amado Nervo. Shortly after ASU made its announcement, the Nicaraguan novelist Sergio Ramírez published an article in which he denounced the letters as fake.

JANUARY 21, 2013

Dear Sergio:

Your depiction—in *Margarita,*
How Beautiful The Sea—
of my homecoming to León in 1907

once again filled my arms with bouquets
that dampened my silk suit, baskets of flowers
and fruit, which I accepted with a nod

though leaving them in the hands of my entourage,
a cambric handkerchief wiping the sweat
dripping down my face and neck.

And as I opened a path for myself, village
folk pressing around, their lips at my sleeves,
a little boy with curly hair led the way

clutching the flag of Nicaragua.
I loved how you had Momotombo,
years later in 1916, blow—

moments after I drew my last breath,
the volcano producing a deep rumbling,
sending people into the streets,

a spatter of sparks lighting the sky.
I wasn't aware (of course) of what came next—
your novel placing me there, in that room:

the doctor's scalpel blinking like a star
in the moment it traced the incision
on my forehead, my scalp folded back, the saw's

fine teeth biting into cranium, he
feverishly snipping ligaments, holding in his hands
my brain, seconds later proclaiming:

"Here it is—the private vessel of the muses!"
More than cringe, I blushed
at being handled with such care.

Perhaps you're surprised by this letter?
You shouldn't be. Anything is possible
in this racket of ours. But artful

is not how I'd describe that piece
you penned last November. You see:
those letters to Amado were real.

I bargained with myself, rewrote them
to preserve them, precisely because I knew
what would happen—you know

as well as I: he would have destroyed them
after reading them: *What will people say?!*
(he with wife and children) held sway . . .

I *was* in New York shortly after New Year's
in 1915 heading home, when I wrote to him
one more time. But you were right

and I'm mildly embarrassed to admit it:
I told a little lie on those sheaths
of Hotel Astor stationery in Times Square:

the poem I enclosed wasn't composed
in Barcelona expressly for him:
it was a piece of juvenalia, I know, but one

I had a soft spot for, and which I re-titled
and dedicated—to him. It was a running joke
between us: sending each other our fluff.

And yet, it's ironic Sergio: thank you
for being complicit, for hinting at
my understory. How did you manage to nail

those final hours? I was indeed lying curled up
on my side, wrapped in a thick, gray blanket, snoring
lightly, my mouth slightly open as my fingers gripped

the silver crucifix that Amado—yes, Amado Nervo—
had given to me in Paris
when we shared that apartment

in Montmartre, and that I always carried
with me. I'd like to think that, somehow,
you knew—and know—this truth.

I'm waiting for the day when you,
the world, stop fighting it. I am
dead, and the dead are very patient.

Love,
Rubén

WINTER HOURS

Look

at him, curled
in a large, plush
chair, wrapped

in sable fur,
fireplace glowing
just beyond, the angora

nosing the fabric
of his shirt,
a porcelain vase

beside the folding
screen, draped
with silk, his eyes

subtle filters
allowing sleep
to seep through. He enters

in silence, takes off his
gray coat, pecks
the slender rose

of his face, a fleur-de-lis
—Amado wakes, smiles, snow
general over París.

after Rubén Darío's "De invierno"

Bay Area Rapid Transit

. . . you in my
Kodak memory
he says, looking

up at her from his seat—
his speech from the beginning deliberate
and slow, touching

her with it
while she, who seems at ease,
touches him back—*is that*

so . . . and where you
getting off at? . . . shifting
her weight from foot

to foot, one hand above, her fingers
curled around the bar . . .
—*You don't need it*

was his opening,
having noticed the compact piece
of equipment, *The Body*

Maker . . . while the other
is at her thigh, forming
a hook around the handle

of her see-through
shopping bag

POEM BEGINNING WITH A FRAGMENT
OF ANDRÉS MONTOYA

the taco vender/reciting/darío/in a moment/of passion—
I swear it was him that night, 2012, late July...
We were hoofing it down Guadalupe looking

for a dive—how many were we and who? He'd hauled
his camión from Fresno to Austin, swapping one
heat for another. La princesa está triste . . . ¿Qué

tendrá la princesa? Was it you, Lety, gritando "Let's
do Hole in the Wall, or is it the Local with that
taco truck in the back!?"—I swear it was him

that night, 2012, late July... We were seated
around two, three mesas in the open air talking
shop: Era un aire suave, de pausados giros:

"You're from the Mission?" "Yeah." "¿Y eres
Nica?" "Sí."—"¡Que cool!" ... We were hoofing
it down Guadalupe looking for a dive—and found

carne asada, barbacoa, carnitas, al pastor

    for Leticia Hernández-Linares

CREED

I soared across the sky to peer
down at you all.
Each flap bringing me closer—
your idea of heaven.
No, I don't believe.
My prayer's a sheet of ice
scrutinized
by unforgiving heat.
Now my words are air.
Without remorse I compose—
hold you inside me.
Saints are sliced in four.
I sing the rhythm of their days.
Spirit endures, soft
as a kiss, calling
us to chorus, to convene
antepasados en el desierto.
To swallow what they teach.

for Carmen Calatayud

V

My Rubén

notes on a trajectory, a controversy

I

La princesa está triste . . . ¿qué tendrá la princesa?
Los suspiros se escapan de su boca de fresa

"Tell me the one about the princess," I'd say, and she'd readily utter these two lines. Except for a set of aqua-blue encyclopedias, ours wasn't a household replete with books. And yet, during my childhood, this arrangement of words about a sad princess sighing through strawberry lips would float free from my mother's own lips. Standing at an ironing board, on the couch watching a telenovela, seated at the kitchen table removing tiny pebbles from a pile of uncooked pinto beans. Nothing kept her from retrieving this poem—one she had to learn in the early forties as a school girl in Nicaragua, though she never went beyond the sixth grade. You might say, then, that my mother's favorite Rubén Darío poem had become part of her DNA, her breath—something she passed on to me.

In high school, when I sought these poems out, it was the English translations of Lysander Kemp I had to read. I don't recall, however, reading his versions with as much delight as listening to my mother. Although I grew up speaking and understanding spoken Spanish, I was illiterate until I began to study the language formally at UC Berkeley.

My first meaningful experience as a reader of Spanish was when, living in Spain as a student, I set out to read Ian Gibson's two-volume biography of Federico García Lorca. In volume one, in a section where he is making light of the profound impact Rubén Darío's work had on the young Lorca, Gibson quotes, in full, a Darío masterpiece: "Lo fatal." I was finally able to properly experience what all the fuss was about.

Because I was aspiring to write poems of my own, I wondered how "Lo fatal" might sound in English. It was a poem, for the most part, bereft of images. Its power resided in its gorgeous rhythms and rhymes and, I think, its arresting theme. It was a poem that didn't lend itself, in my view, to conventional modes of translation. Not knowing any better, I decided to re-cast the piece as I saw fit.

I deployed very short lines, ignoring the poem's original sonnet-like shape. The result was a draft of what became the second poem in section two of this book: "The Inevitable." It remained, for many years, my one and only attempt at what I'm certain would be considered blasphemous in most translation circles. Looking back, it was personal: I was the son of Nicaraguan immigrants who heard Darío as a child. I was giving myself permission to play with Rubén, *my* Rubén.

My early efforts at literary translation were with the work of the late Francisco X. Alarcón; the homoerotic sonnets of Federico García Lorca; and the avant-garde verse of Lorca's contemporary, Gerardo Diego—the latter as my thesis while pursuing an M.A. in Hispanic Civilization through New York University ("NYU in Spain"). This encompassed the late eighties to the early nineties in Madrid.

It wasn't until my first semester as an MFA candidate in creative writing that I returned to Rubén Darío. Context meant everything. My first workshop at Notre Dame was a revelation. John Matthias organized the course with translation as the lens through which we would view and do everything. Matthias's workshop made manifest something another former teacher, Thom Gunn, had said in an undergraduate workshop at Berkeley. Paraphrasing: "Reading, as experiences go, can also serve as a source of inspiration for our poems."

Matthias's workshop made possible the other nine Darío versions and riffs dispersed throughout sections one through four of this book, not to mention a number of other pieces that splice lines and fragments from other poetic texts. The reader, at this point, might be asking what, precisely, did he have us do? Mostly, he assigned, and had us thoroughly discuss, certain crucial texts. George Steiner's *After Babel* was one. Robert Lowell's *Imitations* was another. And then, simply, we were free to pursue our passions. For me it was a matter of testing certain ideas and methods out on Rubén Darío during those fifteen weeks in the fall of 2001. What do I mean? Well, this notion that the source text—a poem in Spanish for instance—could be a *vehicle* for writing a poem in English, one closely inspired by the original—or, to render the source poem into a very liberal English version of the original. Notice: I'm avoiding the term "translation," its traditional sense. It was the beginning, I think, of my blossoming interest and preoccupation in works of art inspired by other works of art. In this first phase, it was a matter of one text begetting another. As the years progressed I began to grow increasingly interested, obsessed even, in the phenomena of the visual and plastic arts becoming the springboard for literary art. But for the matter at hand: most of my Darío versions in *After Rubén* had their start in Matthias's workshop.

II

The nameless storefront, hours north of San Francisco, looked abandoned: the plate glass windows were covered, from the inside, with newspaper—like a business gone bust on the town's main strip. The town was Corning, just south of Red Bluff. I tapped the glass firmly with a nickel, and waited. The door opened. The man standing before me was bleary-eyed, his hair gray, abundant, disheveled, looking as if he'd just crawled out of bed, though it was two in the afternoon. He was wearing corduroys and a wrinkled shirt—a turtleneck. "Hola, papá," I said. My father opened the door further, gestured for me to step inside. When he shut the door everything went dark. At a distance, some light seeped through what looked to be a wide curtain hung from a cord that spanned the width of the room. *The Price Is Right* blared from a television behind it. My eyes adjusted: some empty display cases immediately off to the side—the kind you see in a jewelry store. I discerned bulging bags piled high in the corners to the left and right. I caught a shadow slinking by: a cat. I noticed sparsely populated clothing racks. "Let me show you around," he said and began to walk away. I followed him down a pathway of stuff—boxes mostly. Once I was past the glass cases, the low-ceilinged room seemed to open up and there were beds, three of them, up against the wall on the right. There were dressers, too, placed in between the beds as if they were functioning as low walls—as if each bed and dresser constituted a makeshift "room" in that storefront-turned-living space. My father approached what I saw were hanging bedsheets; he slipped his hand into a seam and swept one of them aside like a stage curtain, and stepped into the light.

In the months after my mother's death in January of 1997, I paid my father two visits up in Corning, each lasting ten days. One evening, during the first visit, while strolling down the main drag on our way to Safeway, the subject of poetry came up and he began to tell me about *his* favorite Rubén Darío poem: "Los motivos del lobo." I didn't know the poem and so listened intently as my father paraphrased the story from Saint Francis of Assisi's life, as depicted by Darío— how he tamed the wolf that had been terrorizing an Italian village; how the wolf lapsed back to being a wild animal; how Saint Francis, sad at this turn of events, began to say the Our Father to end the poem. When I returned to Spain that June, I tracked the poem down, and marveled at it, admiring how Darío had taken a well-known, popular, perhaps even sentimental myth—and complicated it, making it more interesting, nuanced, problematic.

Why hadn't I attempted to render this poem into English during that seminal workshop with John Matthias? At six pages, perhaps I deemed it too long for my semester project; perhaps I wanted to attempt shorter Darío poems first, and leave the wolf poem for later. In fact, it wasn't until 2002 or 2003 that I took the wolf poem with me to Europe on a week-long, self-directed writing retreat. The task I'd set for myself was one, and one only. "Los motivos del lobo" became, in Dublin, Ireland, "The Man and the Wolf"—a free verse poem in forty-seven tercets and a single final line. Like a number of the pieces in this book, it became one of my *after Rubén Darío* poems. Before finding a more permanent home here, "The Man and the Wolf" took up residence in 2006 in *Evensong: Contemporary American Poets on Spirituality*. In my headnote for that volume, I spoke about how the poem became a kind of metaphor for those twenty days I spent with my father in the wake of my mother's death. Twenty years later, it's still a poem I immediately associate with him. Increasingly, I've come to think of it as his gift to me—my inheritance.

III

[I]f we sanitize, compromise, or self-censor, we are only pulling out our wings.
—*Rigoberto González*

The e-invitation landed in my inbox in mid-November of 2012. It began: "Dear Writer Friend, I want to let you know that I'm beginning—and ending—a literary magazine. A one-issue deal, that issue ending up solely in the hands of the writers contained in it . . . The magazine will be called *Forward to Velma*, and will be epistolary: one of letters, correspondence."

Considering the source of the invitation, and how interesting I deemed its parameters, I immediately thought, *Yes—I'm in*. Around this time, I'd also become aware of a press release from earlier in the month titled, "ASU Libraries acquires rare manuscripts of Nicaraguan poet Rubén Darío." One paragraph leapt off the page:

"The documents have already begun to alter the scholarship on Darío. The peer-reviewed '*Bulletin of Spanish Studies*,' a prestigious academic journal from the United Kingdom, has published an article by [Alberto] Acereda in its September 2012 issue based on the letters found in the ASU collection. The article, 'Nuestro más profundo y sublime secreto: Los amores transgresores entre Rubén Darío y Amado Nervo,' reveals for the first time a secret romantic relationship between Darío and famed Mexican poet Amado Nervo (1870–1919)."

The revelation felt seismic. Up until then, my gay literary mentors had been unapologetically "out." Or, even if they weren't direct mentors, were "out" as far as how public consciousness perceived them. But Rubén Darío? He wasn't part of *that* pantheon. He wasn't Hart Crane or Oscar Wilde. He wasn't, for that matter, Amado Nervo himself, about whom my gay literary friends in Spain had let *that* penny drop over twenty years ago.

Darío's persona had always seemed somewhat anguished to me, tormented even; and so this revelation added a poignant, if bittersweet, sheen to his biography. Is it possible that I saw something of myself in that anguish—was that why this revelation struck me as it did?

I was indeed a skinny, insecure boy with a skateboard in the years before I entered high school—as the first poem in this book hints at. My refuge, as I intimated in the essay that punctuated my last book, *Glow of Our Sweat*, was schoolwork and sports. Skateboarding was another. I was a connoisseur of sorts—not acquiring a board that was ready-made, but putting one together part by part: a fiberglass deck, a particular brand of trucks, polyurethane wheels. A nerd of the genre in other words. My red zephyr with its black, custom-fit grip tape was my ride—for exploring San Francisco streets I wouldn't otherwise venture down, on foot.

Once, I rode past a frame shop that also carried, I discovered, greeting cards aimed at a particular audience of the masculine persuasion. I found myself browsing, now and then, plucking cards from the rack to quench a certain gaze. But that afternoon in 1980 when I spotted my mother across the street as I exited the shop, board in hand, marked my last visit. In my essay, I said it like this: "And in darker moments, this thought: *I'd rather be dead than have anyone, friend or stranger, learn my secret.*"

Through one of my contacts at ASU, I managed to land an e-introduction to Alberto Acereda. He was kind enough to send me a PDF of his eye-opening article, which I promptly devoured. It included the nine letters Darío had written to Nervo. The last one was penned on January 12, 1915. The Hotel Astor near Times Square had provided stationery. This final letter left no doubt about the nature of the bond between the two Spanish-language poets.

When I'd first received that invitation to submit a piece to *Forward to Velma*, it occurred to me that this Darío-Nervo story was ripe with possibility in terms of subject matter. After reading Acereda's article, possibility became certainty: I knew what kind of poem I would draft.

Or so I thought. Sergio Ramírez, a prominent Nicaraguan writer, soon weighed in, online, with a thousand-word piece in which he denounced the nine letters as false. His argument, at first glance, seemed plausible, pointing out some erroneous dates, questions to do with Darío's handwriting, other incidentals.

If my initial impulse was to pen a poem in the voice of Rubén Darío addressed to his secret lover, this latest twist spurred an imaginative leap in a different direction. The epistle would still be in Darío's voice, but it would be a letter addressed to this skeptical public figure—from the grave. I should say, for the record, that I love Ramírez's work, one novel in particular in which, it so happens, he movingly depicts two periods from Rubén Darío's life, including his final moments. If I haven't made it explicitly clear, reading was another refuge during those lonely years.

Including the summer I fell in love with Frank O'Hara. It was immediately after my first year at Cal—*before* I enrolled in my first writing workshop and concurrently joined the staff of the *Berkeley Poetry Review*. During the spring semester of 1985, I discovered that the course offerings that June included a class called Literature and the Arts. The topic was American poetry and painting—specifically, cubism and abstract expressionism. We'd be reading William Carlos Williams, Gertrude Stein, John Ashbery, and Frank O'Hara. I enrolled in a New York minute, not really cognizant of how lucky I was. The instructor was the late James E.B. Breslin, who would go on to write a seminal biography of Mark Rothko, but who I would mostly know from his *From Modern to Contemporary: American Poetry, 1945–1965*—one of my favorite books *about* poetry. I liked all the poets we read that summer well enough. But Frank O'Hara's exuberance and verve just bowled me over, turning him into one of my first gay literary heroes.

I commuted to class from San Francisco that summer, and one afternoon, riding BART, absently flipping through the dog-eared pages of *Selected Poems* with its Larry Rivers nude of O'Hara on the cover, I casually read the editor's bio in the back and saw that Donald Allen "resided in San Francisco." As soon as I got home I grabbed the phone book and confirmed in the White Pages that Allen lived on Grand View—a thirty or so minute walk from my home.

The neatly typed beige postcard read: "Dear Mr. Aragon: Thank you for your lovely letter. I no longer edit verse. I would be delighted to meet you. My phone number is 824-7211. Sincerely, Donald Allen." When the appointed day arrived, I stepped out onto the sidewalk on Fair Oaks, turned left and walked up the hill to the corner, turning right on 24th and proceeded to walk up another hill, crossing Dolores into the heart of Noe Valley, continuing for ten blocks, past Castro, Diamond, Douglass, Hoffman, turning right on Grand View and walking down a slope and then up, until I reached the address of the nondescript apartment building. I rang the bell, was buzzed in. Greeting me at the door was a man of seventy or so, medium-build with a trim moustache and a head of beautiful white hair, wearing a cardigan. He invited me to take a seat on his immaculate sofa, his apartment exquisitely arranged, antique pieces here and there. He served coffee and cake, asked if I cared to listen to music. He put on something classical, in a volume discreet enough to permit conversation. I tentatively asked about Frank O'Hara. Allen recounted with humor and affection that Frank loved sharing stories from his time in the Navy, details of which he chose not to reveal, and which I was too shy to ask for. I'd been sitting there for about an hour when Allen rose, disappeared, and came back with two books he was kind enough to sign. *Standing Still and Walking in New York*, featuring a striking photograph of O'Hara and Larry Rivers with arms crossed, leaning on a building while appearing to fix their gaze on something in front of them. And *Frank O'Hara: Early Writing*, in white script against green and featuring a very young O'Hara in profile looking to the left, with his slightly crooked nose—broken, according to Allen, from a boxing match in his youth. It was now my cue to leave. I said goodbye to Donald Allen, the legendary editor of American poetry. I was nineteen. And very much still in the closet.

As I found myself quietly immersed in this Nicaraguan polemic involving Rubén Darío's letters, what inevitably came to mind was Spain's often fraught relationship with *its* national poetry treasure: Federico García Lorca. In 2009 Ian Gibson, pre-eminent biographer and scholar, offered this on the occasion of *Lorca y el mundo gay*, his fourth and final book on the Andalusian poet: "Spain couldn't accept that the greatest Spanish poet of all time was homosexual. Homophobia existed on both sides of the civil war." Was there a similar dynamic unfolding with Nicaragua's national poetry treasure?

I wrote and submitted my poem to *Forward to Velma*, titling it "January 21, 2013"—a piece that went on to occupy its place in the privately published and distributed literary magazine, after which it appeared in a public print journal, and then an online magazine, and then again in an anthology of Central American writing in the U.S., and then my fourth chapbook, before finally settling into the pages of *After Rubén*.

In the months that followed, I wondered if there would be a response to the charge that these letters were falsified. That summer I had my answer. In its 2013 edition, *Siglo diecinueve (Literatura hispánica)*, a peer-reviewed annual edited in Spain, published "Los manuscritos Darianos de Arizona. Autenticidad de la colección y apostillas a las cartas a Amado Nervo" by none other than Alberto Acereda. As with his piece published in *Bulletin of Spanish Studies*, once I was able to land a PDF of the *Siglo diecinueve* article, I carefully read it, and re-read it, with much interest.

Acereda prosecuted his case over the course of thirty-one pages, offering detailed context for every one of the nine letters, including reports of how maps and almanacs of early 19th century Madrid and New York were studied in order to pin down the geographical circumstances of each and every letter.

Although he didn't explicitly claim homophobia as the motivation for the pushback this new branch of Darío scholarship was encountering, he seemed to insinuate it. One allegation he cited was that there was an error in a date in one of the letters. All throughout Darío scholarship, Acereda countered, where documents in Darío's own hand had played a central role, there had been a number of instances where scholars had come upon discrepancies and/or errors. In those cases, scholars were often able to correct, amend, or offer plausible explanations, using other primary sources and cross references to bolster their conclusions. In *none* of those cases, Acereda observed, had the authenticity of the Darío manuscripts been called into question. It had always been understood, and accepted, that artists—human beings after all—sometimes got their dates mixed up. What is more, he argued, why would a deliberate falsifier get dates wrong if the aim was to have the falsified document appear authentic?

Doesn't it speak volumes that rigorous, peer-reviewed literary scholarship is being met with the Documents-Must-Be-Fake argument on the first occasion that, ostensibly, said scholarship points to the subject having been involved in a same-sex liaison?

What's been detailed here unfolded back in 2012 and 2013. But, as if to underscore that we continue to live in an era in which homophobia can still manifest itself as merely another point of view, someone as recently as last spring casually asserted to me that this Darío-Nervo business was little more than an effort to *ensuciar* Rubén Darío's name. The verb *ensuciar* roughly means to dirty or soil. The insidiousness of that verb, how it was used, caught me off guard.

In a conversation with noted poet and critic Rigoberto González last year, in the aftermath of losing our mutual mentor, Francisco X. Alarcón, González noted with dismay what he perceived, in some public pronouncements, as a certain de-emphasizing if not outright muting of Alarcón's gay identity in deference to his Chicanx identity—thereby undercutting the very lesson Alarcón had always strived to impart throughout his life: that one's ethnic identity should not temper or dilute one's LGBTQ identity; that both can and should equally co-exist, as they unapologetically have, for example, with González himself.

The Rubén Darío of my childhood, as represented by my mother's favorite poem and its depiction of a princess, is the innocent strand of a braid—one that elevates fantasy and the imagination. My father's Darío, whose emblematic gesture is the loss of that innocence in favor of life's harsher realities, as told in the re-imagined story of Saint Francis' wolf, is the second strand of this braid. *These* are what my mother and father passed on to me.

I'd like to think the Rubén Darío of the nine letters to Amado Nervo completes this braid. In the words of Alberto Acereda, at the end of his piece in *Bulletin of Spanish Studies*, "These letters offer us a Darío and Nervo who are even more human, more passionate than what we imagined . . ." In fact, I would suggest that those who resist this third strand suffer from a deficit of the imagination—preferring to keep Rubén Darío in a more tidy, less complicated box. Call it a coffin.

The question to be answered in the years to come is: Will it be the Rubén Darío of this completed braid that fully blossoms, that comes to occupy, without controversy, his place alongside Federico García Lorca, Luis Cernuda, Vicente Aleixandre, Amado Nervo, José Lezama Lima, and Francisco X. Alarcón, to name half a dozen Spanish-language poets, as among this linguistic tradition's distinguished mariposa voices?

With that, Rubén will have the last word—though with a caveat. Darío took his last breath while gripping a rosary given to him by Amado Nervo. And yet he chose *not* to include in an anthology of his work—whose selection he himself oversaw—a sonnet titled "Amado Nervo." Was it, perhaps, a conflicted effort to draw attention away from what may have been the love of his life?

Regardless, here is a snippet, addressed, perhaps, to Nervo himself:

Generoso y sutil como una mariposa,
encuentra en mí la miel de que soy capaz,
y goza en mí la dulce fragancia de la rosa.

Both ample and nuanced as a butterfly,
in me you'll find the nectar I can become,
enjoy in me the sweet scent of a rose.

in memory of Francisco X. Alarcón

August 2018
Torquay, U.K.

Appendix

Ten poems by Rubén Darío

ALLÁ LEJOS

Buey que vi en mi niñez echando vaho un día
bajo el nicaragüense sol de encendidos oros,
en la hacienda fecunda, plena de la armonía
del trópico; paloma de los bosques sonoros
del viento, de las hachas, de pájaros y toros
salvajes, yo os saludo, pues sois la vida mía.

Pesado buey, tú evocas la dulce madrugada
que llamaba a la ordeña de la vaca lechera,
cuando era mi existencia toda blanca y rosada;
y tú, paloma arrulladora y montañera,
significas en mi primavera pasada
todo lo que hay en la divina Primavera.

LO FATAL

Dichoso el árbol que es apenas sensitivo,
y más la piedra dura porque esa ya no siente,
pues no hay dolor más grande que el dolor de ser vivo,
ni mayor pesadumbre que la vida consciente.

Ser, y no saber nada, y ser sin rumbo cierto,
y el temor de haber sido y un futuro terror . . .
Y el espanto seguro de estar mañana muerto,
y sufrir por la vida y por la sombra y por

lo que no conocemos y apenas sospechamos,
y la carne que tienta con sus frescos racimos,
y la tumba que aguarda con sus fúnebres ramos,
¡y no saber adónde vamos,
ni de dónde venimos! . . .

A Roosevelt

¡Es con voz de la Biblia, o verso de Walt Whitman,
que habría que llegar hasta ti, Cazador!
¡Primitivo y moderno, sencillo y complicado,
con algo de Washington y cuatro de Nemrod!

Eres los Estados Unidos,
eres el futuro invasor
de la América ingenua que tiene sangre indígena,
que aun reza a Jesucristo y aun habla español.

Eres soberbio y fuerte ejemplar de tu raza;
eres culto, eres hábil; te opones a Tolstoy.
Y domando caballos, o asesinando tigres,
eres un Alejandro-Nabucodonosor.
(Eres un professor de energía,
como dicen los locos de hoy.)

Crees que la vida es incendio,
que el progreso es erupción;
en donde pones la bala
el porvenir pones.
                    No.

Los Estados Unidos son potentes y grandes.
Cuando ellos se estremecen hay un hondo temblor
que pasa por las vértebras enormes de los Andes.
Si clamáis, se oye como el rugir del león.
Ya Hugo a Grant lo dijo: "Las estrellas son vuestras".
(Apenas brilla, alzándose, el argentino sol
y la estrella chilena se levanta . . .) Sois ricos.
Juntáis al culto de Hércules el culto de Mammón;
y alumbrando el camino de la fácil conquista,
la Libertad levanta su antorcha en Nueva-York.

Mas la América nuestra, que tenía poetas
desde los viejos tiempos de Netzahualcoyotl,
que ha guardado las huellas de los pies del gran Baco,
que el alfabeto pánico en un tiempo aprendió;
que consultó los astros, que conoció la Atlántida,
cuyo nombre nos llega resonando en Platón,
que desde los remotos momentos de su vida
vive de luz, de fuego, de perfume, de amor,
la América del grande Moctezuma, del Inca,
la América fragante de Cristóbal Colón,
la América católica, la América española,
la América en que dijo el noble Guatemoc:
"Yo no estoy en un lecho de rosas"; esa América
que tiembla de huracanes y que vive de Amor;
hombres de ojos sajones y alma bárbara, vive.
Y sueña. Y ama, y vibra; y es la hija del Sol.
Tened cuidado. ¡Vive la América española!,
hay mil cachorros sueltos del León Español.
Se necesitaría, Roosevelt, ser por Dios mismo,
el Riflero terrible y el fuerte Cazador,
para poder teneros en vuestra férreas garras.

Y, pues contáis con todo, falta una cosa: ¡Dios!

LOS MOTIVOS DEL LOBO

El varón que tiene corazón de lis,
alma de querube, lengua celestial,
el mínimo y dulce Francisco de Asís,
está con un rudo y torvo animal,
bestia temerosa, de sangre y de robo,
las fauces de furia, los ojos de mal:
el lobo de Gubbia, el terrible lobo.
Rabioso ha asolado los alrededores,
cruel ha deshecho todos los rebaños;
devoró corderos, devoró pastores,
y son incontables sus muertes y daños.

Fuertes cazadores armados de hierros
fueron destrozados. Los duros colmillos
dieron cuenta de los más bravos perros,
como de cabritos y de corderillos.

Francisco salió:
al lobo buscó
en su madriguera.
Cerca de la cueva encontró a la fiera
enorme, que al verle se lanzó feroz
contra él. Francisco, con su dulce voz,
alzando la mano,
al lobo furioso dijo: "¡Paz, hermano
lobo!" El animal
contempló al varón de tosco sayal;
dejó su aire arisco,
cerró las abiertas fauces agresivas,
y dijo: "¡Está bien, hermano Francisco!"
"¡Cómo!" exclamó el santo. ¿Es ley que tú vivas
de horror y de muerte?
¿La sangre que vierte
tu hocico diabólico, el duelo y espanto

que esparces, el llanto
de los campesinos, el grito, el dolor
de tanta criatura de Nuestro Señor,
no han de contener tu encono infernal?
¿Vienes del infierno?
¿Te ha infundido acaso su rencor eterno
Luzbel o Belial?"
Y el gran lobo, humilde: "¡Es duro el invierno,
y es horrible el hambre! En el bosque helado
no hallé qué comer; y busqué el ganado,
y en veces comí ganado y pastor.
¿La sangre? Yo vi más de un cazador
sobre su caballo, llevando el azor
al puño; o correr tras el jabalí,
el oso o el ciervo; a más de uno vi
mancharse de sangre, herir, torturar,
de las roncas trompas al sordo clamor,
a los animales de Nuestro Señor.
Y no era por hambre, que iban a cazar."
Francisco responde: "En el hombre existe
mala levadura.
Cuando nace viene con pecado. Es triste.
Mas el alma simple de la bestia es pura.
Tú vas a tener
desde hoy qué comer.
Dejarás en paz
rebaños y gente en este país.
¡Qué Dios melifique tu ser montaraz!"
"Está bien hermano Francisco de Asís."
"Ante el Señor, que todo ata y desata,
en fe de promesa tiéndame la pata."
El lobo tendió la pata al hermano
de Asís, que a su vez le alargó la mano.
Fueron a la aldea. La gente veía

y lo que miraba casi no creía.
Tras el religioso iba el lobo fiero,
y, baja la testa, quieto le seguía
como un can de casa, o como un cordero.

Francisco llamó la gente a la plaza
y allí predicó.
Y dijo: "He aquí una amable caza.
El hermano lobo viene conmigo;
me juró no ser ya nuestro enemigo,
y no repetir su ataque sangriento.
Vosotros, en cambio, daréis su alimento
a la pobre bestia de Dios." "¡Así sea!",
contestó la gente toda de la aldea.
Y luego, en señal
de contentamiento
movió testa y cola el buen animal,
y entró con Francisco de Asís al convento.

Algún tiempo estuvo el lobo tranquilo
en el santo asilo.
Sus bastas orejas los salmos oían
y los claros ojos se le humedecían.
Aprendió mil gracias y hacía mil juegos
cuando a la cocina iba con los legos.
Y cuando Francisco su oración hacía,
el lobo las pobres sandalias lamía.
Salía a la calle,
iba por el monte, descendía al valle,
entraba a las casas y le daban algo
de comer. Mirábanle como a un manso galgo.
Un día, Francisco se ausentó. Y el lobo
dulce, el lobo manso y bueno, el lobo probo,
desapareció, tornó a la montaña,

y recomenzaron su aullido y su saña.
Otra vez sintióse el temor, la alarma,
pues la bestia fiera
no dio treguas a su furor jamás,
como si tuviera
fuegos de Moloch y de Satanás.

Cuando volvió al pueblo el divino santo,
todos lo buscaron con quejas y llanto,
y con mil querellas dieron testimonio
de lo que sufrían y perdían tanto
por aquel infame lobo del demonio.

Francisco de Asís se puso severo.
Se fue a la montaña
a buscar al falso lobo carnicero.
Y junto a su cueva halló a la alimaña.
"En nombre del Padre del sacro universo,
conjúrate", dijo, "¡oh lobo perverso!,
a que me respondas: ¿Por qué has vuelto al mal?
Contesta. Te escucho."
Como en sorda lucha, habló el animal,
la boca espumosa y el ojo fatal:
"Hermano Francisco, no te acerques mucho . . .
Yo estaba tranquilo allá, en el convento,
al pueblo salía,
y si algo me daban estaba contento,
y manso comía.
Mas empecé a ver que en todas las casas
estaban la envidia, la saña, la ira,
y en todos los rostros ardían las brasas
de odio, de lujuria, de infamia y mentira.
Hermanos a hermanos hacían la guerra,
perdían los débiles, ganaban los malos,

hembra y macho eran como perro y perra,
y un buen día todos me dieron de palos.
Me vieron humilde, lamía las manos
y los pies. Seguía tus sagradas leyes,
todas las criaturas eran mis hermanos,
los hermanos hombres, los hermanos bueyes,
hermanas estrellas y hermanos gusanos.
Y así, me apalearon y me echaron fuera,
y su risa fue como un agua hirviente,
y entre mis entrañas revivió la fiera,
y me sentí lobo malo de repente;
mas siempre mejor que esa mala gente.
Y recomencé a luchar aquí,
a me defender y a me alimentar,
como el oso hace, como el jabalí,
que para vivir tiene que matar.
Déjame en el monte, déjame en el risco,
déjame existir en mi libertad,
vete a tu convento, hermano Francisco,
sigue tu camino y tu santidad."

El santo de Asís no le dijo nada.
Le miró con una profunda mirada,
y partió con lágrimas y con desconsuelos,
y habló al Dios eterno con su corazón.
El viento del bosque llevó su oración,
que era: "Padre nuestro, que estás en los cielos . . ."

CARACOL

A Antonio Machado

En la playa he encontrado un caracol de oro
macizo y recamado de las perlas más finas;
Europa le ha tocado con sus manos divinas
cuando cruzó las ondas sobre el celeste toro.

He llevado a mis labios el caracol sonoro
y he suscitado el eco de las dianas marinas,
le acerqué a mis oídos y las azules minas
me han contado en voz baja su secreto tesoro.

Así la sal me llega de los vientos amargos
que en sus hinchadas velas sintió la nave Argos
cuando amaron los astros el sueño de Jasón;

y oigo un rumor de olas y un incognito acento
y un profundo oleaje y un misterioso viento . . .
(El caracol la forma tiene de un corazón.)

WALT WHITMAN

En su país de hierro vive el gran viejo,
bello como un patriarca, sereno y santo.
Tiene en la arruga olímpica de su entrecejo
algo que impera y vence con noble encanto.

Su alma del infinito parece espejo;
son sus cansados hombros dignos del manto;
y con arpa labrada de un roble añejo
como un profeta nuevo canta su canto.

Sacerdote, que alimenta soplo divino,
anuncia en el futuro, tiempo mejor.
Dice al águila: "¡Vuela!"; "¡Boga!", al marino,

y ¡Trabaja!", al robusto trabajador.
¡Así va ese poeta por su camino
con su soberbio rostro de emperador!

Yo persigo una forma...

Yo persigo una forma que no encuentra mi estilo,
botón de pensamiento que busca ser la rosa;
se anuncia con un beso que en mis labios se posa
al abrazo imposible de la Venus de Milo.

Adornan verdes palmas el blanco perstilo;
los astros me han predicho la vision de la Diosa;
y en mi alma reposa la luz como reposa
el ave de la luna sobre un lago tranquilo.

Y no hallo sino la palabra que huye,
la iniciación melódica que de la flauta fluye
y la barca del sueño que en el espacio boga;

y bajo la ventana de mi Bella-Durmiente,
el sollozo continuo del chorro de la fuente
y el cuello del gran cisne blanco que me interroga.

SINFONÍA EN GRIS MAYOR

El mar como un vasto cristal azogado
refleja la lámina de un cielo de zinc;
lejanas bandadas de pájaros manchan
el fondo bruñido de pálido gris.

El sol como vidrio redondo y opaco
con paso de enfermo camina al cenit;
el viento marino descansa en la sombra
teniendo de almohada su negro clarín.

Las ondas que mueven su vientre de plomo
debajo del muelle parecen gemir.
Sentado en un cable, fumando su pipa,
está un marinero pensando en las playas
de un vago, lejano, brumoso país.

Es viejo ese lobo. Tostaron su cara
los rayos de fuego del sol del Brasil;
los recios tifones del mar de la China
le han visto bebiendo su frasco de gin.

La espuma impregnada de yodo y salitre
ha tiempo conoce su roja nariz,
sus crespos cabellos, sus bíceps de atleta,
su gorra de lona, su blusa de dril.

En medio del humo que forma el tabaco
ve el viejo el lejano, brumoso país,
adonde una tarde caliente y dorada
tendidas las velas partió el bergantín . . .

La siesta del trópico. El lobo se aduerme.
Ya todo lo envuelve la gama del gris.
Parece que un suave enorme esfumino
del curvo horizonte borrara el confín.

La siesta del trópico. La vieja cigarra
ensaya su ronca guitarra senil,
y el grillo preludia su solo monótono
en la única cuerda que está en su violin.

Triste, muy tristemente...

Un día estaba yo triste, muy tristemente
viendo cómo caía el agua de una fuente;

era la noche dulce y argentina. Lloraba
la noche. Suspiraba la noche. Sollozaba

la noche. Y el crepúsculo en su suave amatista,
diluía la lágrima de un misterioso artista.

Y ese artista era yo, misterioso y gimiente,
que mezclaba mi alma al chorro de la fuente.

1916

De invierno

En invernales horas, mired a Carolina.
Medio apelotonada, descansa en el sillón,
envuelta con su abrigo de marta cibelina
y no lejos del fuego que brilla en el salón.

El fino angora blanco junto a ella se reclina,
rozando con su hocico la falda de Alençon,
no lejos de las jarras de porcelana china
que medio oculta un biombo de seda del Japón.

Con sus sutiles filtros la invade un dulce sueño:
entro, sin hacer ruido; dejo mi abrigo gris;
voy a besar su rostro, rosado y halagüeño

como una rosa roja que fuera flor de lis.
Abre los ojos, mírame con su mirada risueño,
y en tanto cae la nieve del cielo de París.

Notes to some of the poems and the essay

I

"2012"

"Untitled" is a silk-screen print by Chicano artist Malaquias Montoya, inspired by the poetry of his late son, Andrés Montoya.

Mandorla: New Writing from the Americas, founded by Roberto Tejada.

Venus in Fur is a two-person play by David Ives set in New York City.

Sex with Strangers is a two-person play by Laura Eason.

Azul . . . is a collection of stories and poems by Rubén Darío, published in Chile in 1888 and considered one of the seminal works of *modernismo*. Among its poems are the sonnets "De invierno" and "Walt Whitman."

PALABRA: A Magazine of Chicano & Latino Literary Art is a magazine founded by elena minor.

Midnight in Paris is a movie written and directed by Woody Allen.

Yuba and Poppie are the names of two family pets—dogs.

My Vocabulary Did This to Me: The Collected Poetry of Jack Spicer was published by University of California Press in 2010.

"Poem with Citations from the O.E.D."

The strategy adopted for this poem is borrowed from Robert Pinsky's "Poem With Refrains."

"Reasons Why She Didn't"

Tipitapa is a municipality in the Managua department of Nicaragua.

"Photo, 1945"

La Prensa, founded in 1926, is Nicaragua's largest circulation daily. The córdoba is Nicaragua's currency.

"Ernesto Cardenal in Berkeley"

In 1982, Ernesto Cardenal gave a poetry reading in Wheeler Auditorium on the UC Berkeley campus.

Francisco Hernández de Córdoba (1475–1526) is reputed as the founder of Nicaragua, and founded two important Nicaraguan cities, Granada and León. Córdoba was an officer of Pedro Arias Dávila. Hernán Cortés and Hernan Ponce de Leon supported Córdoba during the conquest of Nicaragua in 1524 in return for support against Cristóbal de Olid. Pedrarias Dávila considered Córdoba an insurrectionist and a traitor, and finally captured and beheaded him.

II

"1985"

The Contras were U.S.-backed and funded rebel groups active from 1979 to the early 1990s in opposition to the Sandinista government in Nicaragua. The Contras committed a large number of human rights violations. Supporters of the Contras tried to downplay these violations, particularly the Reagan administration.

"Poem with a Phrase of Isherwood"

In 2010, Jan Brewer, Governor of Arizona, signed the Support Our Law Enforcement and Safe Neighborhoods Act, making it "a state crime for illegal immigrants to not have an alien registration document," requiring police "to question people about their immigration status if there is reason." https://www.cbsnews.com/news/arizona-lawmakers-send-immigration-bill-to-gov/

Joe Arpaio is a former Sheriff of Maricopa County, Arizona, from 1993 through 2016. In July 2017 he was convicted of contempt of court, a crime for which he was pardoned by President Donald Trump on August 25, 2017.

"Bay Area Rapid Transit"

Bay Area Rapid Transit (BART) is a rapid transit public transportation system serving the San Francisco Bay Area in California. The heavy rail elevated and subway system connects San Francisco with cities in Alameda, Contra Costa, and San Mateo counties.

"December 31, 1965"

Source material for this poem is taken verbatim from the "Nation" section of *TIME* magazine dated "Friday, December 31, 1965," the date of my birth.

"Lui Minghe Speaks"

On September 9, 2001, a *New York Times* article described the plight of people in China incarcerated under dubious circumstances as a result of China's then "strike hard" campaign. One of those wrongfully convicted to face death, but finally released after lengthy appeals, was a man named Lui Minghe.

"The Century"

The Century, narrated and presented by the late Peter Jennings, is a six-episode television series that reviews some of the most important events of the 20th Century. Each episode takes on two subjects. Episode two, titled "Ultimate Power," explores Hitler's rise to power in Germany and America's race to develop the atom bomb. The physicist was J. Robert Oppenheimer (1904–1967).

III

"We Talk Dogs"

The Yuba River is a tributary of the Feather River in the Sierra Nevada and eastern Sacramento Valley in California.

Cristina Maria Saralegui is a Cuban-born American journalist, television personality, actress and talk show host of the Spanish-language eponymous show, *Cristina*.

American boxer Aaron Pryor (1955–2016) and Nicaraguan boxer Alexis Arguello (1952–2009) fought twice: on November 12, 1982 and September 9, 1983. In the first fight, Arguello attempted to become the first boxer in history to win a world title in four different weight categories. It was dubbed "The Battle of the Champions." Pryor won by TKO in round fourteen. Pryor defeated Arguello again in the rematch by KO in round ten. Both their bouts, especially the first, are considered among the best in boxing history.

"Voices"

Carlos Gardel (1890–1935) was a French Argentine singer, songwriter, composer and actor, and the most prominent figure in the history of tango.

"Caminito" ("little walkway" or "little path" in Spanish) is a street museum and a traditional alley, located in La Boca, a neighborhood of Buenos Aires, Argentina.

Playa Pochomil is one of the more popular beaches on the Pacific Coast, west of Managua, Nicaragua.

IV

"Because They Lived Abroad"

It's well-documented that Rubén Darío and Amado Nervo shared an apartment in the Parisian neighborhood of Montmartre on rue du Faubourg in 1900. My particular source was the notes for Alberto Acereda's article in *Bulletin of Spanish Studies*, which I say more about in my essay, "My Rubén," section V of this book.

"y no saber adonde vamos / ni de donde venimos" is the ending of Rubén Darío's poem, "Lo fatal," from his book, *Cantos de vida y esperanza* (1905).

"Hay golpes en la vida tan fuertes . . . ¡Yo no sé!" is the first and last line from "Los heraldos negros," the title poem from Cesar Vallejo's collection *Los heraldos negros* (1918).

"Voices"

The Cathedral of Saint Matthew the Apostle is located in Washington, D.C., a few doors down from the YMCA at the corner of Rhode Island and Seventeenth Street NW, now demolished.

"January 21, 2013"

This poem paraphrases some passages from Sergio Ramírez's novel, *Margarita, está linda la mar*. The title of the novel is a line from Rubén Darío's poem, "A Margarita Debayle."

On January 21, 2013, Richard Blanco became the first Latinx and the first openly gay poet to read the inaugural poem at a Presidential inauguration, in this case to inaugurate Barack Obama's second term.

"Poem Beginning with a Fragment of Andrés Montoya"

The first line of this poem is a stanza from an Andrés Montoya poem, from his posthumous volume of poetry, *A Jury of Trees* (Bilingual Press/Letras Latinas, 2017).

Leticia Hernández-Linares is a CantoMundo fellow and the author of *Mucha Muchacha, Too Much Girl: Poems* (Tía Chucha Press, 2015).

"Creed"

The "architecture" or "scaffolding" of this poem is borrowed from a poem by Carmen Calatayud in her book *In the Company of Spirits* (Press 53, 2012).

V

"My Rubén"

I.

Félix Rubén García Sarmiento (1867–1916), known as Rubén Darío, was a Nicaraguan poet who initiated the Spanish-American literary movement known as *modernismo* that flourished at the end of the 19th century. Darío has had a great and lasting influence on 20th century Spanish and Latin American literature and journalism. He is the undisputed father of the *modernismo* literary movement (not to be confused with English-language modernism).

The cited rhymed couplet is the first two lines of Rubén Darío's poem "Sonatina," from his collection *Prosas Profanas* from 1896.

Lysander Kemp (1920–1992) worked as a writer, professor, translator, and was head editor of the University of Texas Press from 1966 to 1975. He translated *The Selected Poems of Rubén Darío* (University of Texas Press, 1965).

Ian Gibson is an Irish-born author and Hispanist known for his biographies of the poet Antonio Machado, Salvador Dalí and Federico García Lorca. In 2002, he also published an "autobiography" titled *Yo, Rubén Darío*.

Francisco X. Alarcón (1954–2016) was a Chicano poet and educator. He was one of the few Chicano poets to have gained recognition while writing mostly in Spanish within the United States. He was the author of some twenty books and chapbooks of poetry for adults and children. Among his many awards are the American Book Award and the Fred Cody Lifetime Achievement Award from the Bay Area Book Reviewers Association Award.

Federico García Lorca (1898–1936) was a Spanish poet, playwright, and theatre director. At the outbreak of the Spanish Civil War (1936–1939) he was executed by firing squad by Nationalist forces. Among his poetry collections are *Poeta en Nueva York*, *Romancero gitano*, and *Poema del cante jondo*.

Gerardo Diego (1896–1987) is perhaps the least known poet, outside of Spain, of the renowned Generation of '27, which included, in addition to Lorca, Rafael Alberti, Pedro Salinas, Jorge Guillén and Luis Cernuda, to name a few. Before the Spanish Civil War, Diego had the foresight to edit the groundbreaking and prophetic *Spanish Poetry Anthology 1915–1931*. He was also among the most fervent of his group to explore and embrace the avant-garde tendencies of his time, particularly creationismo. His most well-known collection is from 1925, *Manual de espumas*.

II.

Evensong: Contemporary American Poets on Spirituality (Bottom Dog Press, 2006) was edited by Gerry LaFemina and Chad Prevost.

III.

The epigraph by Rigoberto González is from his essay "Toward a Mariposa Consciousness" in his book *Red-Inked Retablos* (University of Arizona Press, 2013).

Bulletin of Spanish Studies: Hispanic Studies and Researches on Spain, Portugal and Latin America is published by Routledge. The first version of "'Nuestro más profundo y sublime secreto': los amores transgresores entre Rubén Darío y Amado Nervo." was published August 28, 2012.

The essay "Flyer, Closet, Poem" appeared in *Glow of Our Sweat* (Scapegoat Press, 2010).

Sergio Ramírez's online piece titled "El sencillo arte de dejarse de engañar" appeared online in *La Jornada* on November 21, 2012.

"January 21, 2013" appeared in the privately distributed *Forward to Velma*; the print journal, *MiPoesias*; the online journal, *Beltway Poetry Quarterly*; the anthology, *Wandering Song: Central American Writing in the United States* (Tía Chucha Press,

2017); and the limited chapbook *His Tongue a Swath of Sky* (m o m o t o m b i t o, 2019).

The *New Yorker* published "Lorca and the Gay World" about Ian Gibson's book on March 19, 2009, which quotes from an interview with Gibson, first published in *Independent* on March 14, 2009.

Siglo diecinueve (Literature hispánica) is edited by Universitas Castellae in Valladolid, Spain.

Rigoberto González is an award-winning writer and literary activist. He is the author and editor of nineteen books in multiple genres, including poetry, fiction, creative nonfiction, children's literature, and criticism.

In his article "Toward a Mariposa Consciousness: Reimagining Queer Chicano and Latino Identities," published in 2014, literary scholar and poet Daniel Enrique Pérez lays the groundwork of what he calls "a mariposa consciousness, a decolonial site that is grounded in an awareness of the social location, social relations, and history of the mariposa subject." In an e-mail on September 6, 2017, Pérez writes: "I see Mariposa poetics as a genre that includes writers who write in Spanish . . . I view Mariposa theory as a subset of Jotería studies, both have ties to a lengthy history that spans the Americas and Europe."

Publications Acknowledgments

The poems in *After Rubén*, often in earlier versions, have appeared in literary journals, anthologies, community publications, online archives, or as broadsides. I would like to gratefully acknowledge these sources here.

Academy of American Poets archive (online): "Jugglers"; *El Andar*: "The Inevitable"; *Beltway Poetry Quarterly* (online): "January 21, 2013," "2012," "1916," "To George W. Bush" (as "To the President"), "Symphony in Gray," and "*The Century*"; *Borderlands: Texas Poetry Review*: "Voices" (as "My Father's Voice(s)"); *Bordersenses*: "Reasons Why She Didn't"; *Chain*: "Walt" (as "Walt Whitman"); *The Chattahoochee Review*: "Portrait with lines of Montale"; *Chrysalis*: "1916"; *Crab Orchard Review*: "To the Old World" (as "Viejo Mundo") and "We Talk Dogs"(as "Dogs"), as one of two embedded poems in the nonfiction piece, "The Nicaraguan Novel"; *DÁNTA*: "Symphony in Gray"; *Diálogo*: "We Talk Dogs" (as "Perros"); *Electronic Poetry Review* (online): "Poem with Citations from the O.E.D." and "Blister"; *Forward to Velma*: "January 21, 2013"; *Great River Review*: "Academia Escolar," "*Gloria's*" and "Wind & Rain" (as "Of Wind and Rain"); *Heliotrope*: "The Century"; *Jacket* (online): "Nicaragua in a Voice"and "Postcard" (as "View from the Park"); *The Journal*: "Lui Minghe Speaks"; *Jung Journal*: "Helen Speaks"; *KONCH* (online): "Bay Area Rapid Transit"; *The Los Angeles Review*: "Poem Beginning With a Fragment of Andrés Montoya"; *Luna*: "Postcard" (as "View from the Park"); *Mandorla*: "2012," "Voices," "Bay Area Rapid Transit" (as "Poem"), "December 31, 1965," and "Wind & Rain" (as "Of Wind and Rain"); *MiPoesias*: "January 21, 2013"; *The Noe Valley Voice*: "Jugglers" and "Postcard" (as "View from the Park"); *Oxford Review of Books* (online): "Tenochtitlan, 1523"; *PALABRA*: "I Pursue a Shape," "Seashell" (as "Caracol"), and "Winter Hours"; *Pilgrimage*: "Calle Momotombo" and "Poem With a Phrase of Isherwood"; *Poetry Flash*: "1985" (as "Witness"); *Poetry Foundation* archive (online): "Blister"; *Poetry Now*: "Jugglers"; *Public Pool* (online): "Canción," "After Fragments of Juan Felipe Herrera," and "Creed"; *Tertulia* (online): "Nicaragua in a Voice," and "A Wave"; *Written Here*: "Helen Speaks."

"Keough Hall" appeared in the online anthology *No Tender Fences: An anthology of Immigrant & First Generation American Poetry* (2019), which was a fundraiser for the organization, Raices - Texas.

"Far Away" appeared in *HERE: Poems for the Planet* (Cooper Canyon Press, 2019)

"Far Away" was made into a limited edition broadside on the occasion of a reading on April 13, 2019, in Santa Barbara, CA as part of the Mission Poetry Series, curated by Emma Trelles.

"Far Away," "Seashell," "The Man and the Wolf," "To George W. Bush," "January 21, 2013," "Winter Hours," "I Pursue a Shape," and "1916," along with Rubén Darío's Spanish-language originals, made up the limited edition chapbook *His Tongue a Swath of Sky* (*m o m o t o m b i t* o, 2019)

"My Rubén" (essay) appeared in *Crab Orchard Review* in June, 2019.

"Winter Hours," along with the Spanish original, "De invierno," appeared in a brief essay, "Translation as activism: *an updated version of Rubén Darío*" in *Poetry International* (online), summer of 2018.

"2012" appeared in *Nepantla: an anthology for queer poets of color* (Nightboat Books, 2018).

"Keough Hall" was part of the Poetry Foundation's *PoetryNow* audio podcast series in July, 2017.

"We Talk Dogs" (as "Dogs"), "January 21, 2013," and "Blister" appeared in *Wandering Song: Central American Writing in the United States* (Tia Chucha Press, 2017).

"Poem with a Phrase of Isherwood" appeared in *Poetry of Resistance: Voices for Social Justice* (University of Arizona Press, 2016).

"Postcard" appeared in *Not Like the Rest of Us: An Anthology of Contemporary Indiana Writers* (Indiana Writers Center, 2016).

"Poem With A Phrase of Isherwood" appeared in *Cave Canem Anthology XIII.* (Aquarious Press/Willow Books, 2015).

"Lui Minghe Speaks" appeared in *A Face to Meet the Faces: An Anthology of Contemporary Persona Poetry* (University of Akron Press, 2012).

"To George W. Bush" (as "To the President") appeared in *Full Moon On K Street* (Plan B Press, 2010).

"Jugglers" appeared in *Helen Burns Poetry Anthology: New Voices from the Academy of American Poets' University & College Prizes, 1999–2008.* (Academy of American Poets, 2010).

"Blister" appeared in *Mariposas: A Modern Anthology of Queer Latino Poetry* (Floricanto Press, 2008).

"Poem with Citations from the O.E.D" appeared in *Structure & Surprise: Engaging Poetic Turns* (Teachers and Writers Collaborative, 2007).

"Ernesto Cardenal in Berkeley," "Poem with Citations from the O.E.D.," "Portrait with Lines of Montale," "Because They Lived Abroad" (as "Grid"), "To the Old World" (as "Al Viejo Mundo"), and "Far Away" appeared in *The Wind Shifts: New Latino Poetry* (University of Arizona Press, 2007).

"The Man and the Wolf" and "Nicaragua in a Voice" appeared in *Evensong: Contemporary American Poets on Spirituality* (Bottom Dog Press, 2006).

"*The Century*" appeared in *Red, White, & Blues: Poetic Vistas on the Promise of America* (University of Iowa Press, 2004).

"1985" (as "Her Hair") appeared in *Under the Fifth Sun: Latino Literature from California* (Heyday Books, 2002).

"Photo, 1945" appeared in *American Diaspora: Poetry of Displacement* (University of Iowa Press, 2001).

"Postcard" (as "View from the Park"), "Jugglers," and "Photo, 1945" appeared in *Light, Yogurt, Strawberry Milk*, (Chicano Chapbook Series, #26, 1999).

"Symphony in Gray" and "Walt" (as "Walt Whitman") appeared in *Glow of Our Sweat* (Scapegoat Press, 2010).

"The Inevitable" (as "Rubén Darío as Prelude") appeared in *Puerta del Sol* (Bilingual Press, 2005).

"Portrait with lines of Montale" was a Red Dragonfly Press broadside, set by hand by the author and printed on September 21–22, 2007 at the Anderson Center in Red Wing, MN, in an edition of eighty-five.

"Jugglers" won an Academy of American Poets Prize in 1999.

"1985" (as "Witness") won 1st Place in *Mr. Cogito*'s Human Rights Poetry Contest in 1987.

Acknowledgments

Deep gratitude to the following organizations: the Macondo Writers Workshop with special thanks to Sandra Cisneros; CantoMundo, whose workshops yielded a number of the poems in this book; the Dodge Poetry Festival, for their invitation to read at their festival in 2018; Split This Rock, for their invitation to read at their festival in 2010; Red Hen Press and Kate Gale, for inviting me to read at a number of their events over the years; Mesa Refuge with special thanks to Susan Page Tillet, for designating me as the inaugural Poetry Fellow in 2015; the Community of Writers at Squaw Valley with special thanks to Brenda Hillman for inviting me to be a staff poet in 2017; the Institute for Latino Studies at the University of Notre Dame, for being my institutional home since 2003. I'd like to acknowledge and thank my fellow co-founding members of the Poetry Coalition for their camaraderie in recent years. My gratitude to Hank Feenstra for a one-week writers retreat in the Pacific Northwest in 2014. My thanks to Fred Arroyo and Emma Trelles for offering a fresh set of eyes on the manuscript and providing feedback for the "pruning" that *After Rubén* underwent. Special thanks to Michael Dowdy, Juan Felipe Herrera, Carmen Giménez Smith, Cornelius Eady, Ada Limón, John Phillip Santos, and Valerie Martínez for their endorsements. Special thanks to Jose Rodeiro for permission to reproduce his art on the cover. Fellow writers who have been compañero/as and inspirational models of literary citizenship over the years: Fred Arroyo, Naomi Ayala, José Ballesteros, Richard Blanco, Sarah Browning, Carmen Calatayud, Don Cellini, Teri Cross Davis, Blas Falconer, Gina Franco, Carmen Giménez Smith, Rigoberto González, Maria Melendez Kelson, Alexandra Lytton-Regalado, John Matthias, Orlando Menes, Juan J. Morales, Carlos Parada Ayala, Kim Roberts, John Phillip Santos, Emma Trelles, Natalia Treviño, Dan Vera, and Louis Villalba. Other friends who have nourished me: Bill McGrath, Wally Babington, Ken Crocker, Marvin Kuperstein, Roger Carlson, Stan Peabody, Wesley Waite, Gary Hogle, Paul Romero, José Medina, Larry Feinberg, Steve Leahy, Dave Glidden, and George Castillo. Hearfelt thanks to Kate Gale and Mark Cull, with whom I connected in 2009 at the FIL in Guadalajara, Mexico and embarked on multifaceted collaborations, including this book—it's been fun. Special thanks to my family on the West Coast for their unconditional love and support. The essay, "My Rubén" was written on the coast of Devon in Torquay, England: thank you, Mike Cook, for providing a home during the homestretch of this book.

A San Francisco native, **Francisco Aragón** (author) is the son of Nicaraguan immigrants. Upon his return to the U.S. in 1998 after a decade in Spain, Aragón completed degrees in creative writing from UC Davis and the University of Notre Dame. In 2003 he joined the faculty of the University of Notre Dame's Institute for Latino Studies (ILS), where he established Letras Latinas. In 2017, he was a finalist for Split This Rock's Freedom Plow Award for poetry and activism. A CantoMundo fellow and a member of the Macondo Writers' Workshop, he is the author of *Puerta del Sol* (Bilingual Press) and *Glow of Our Sweat* (Scapegoat Press), as well as editor of *The Wind Shifts: New Latino Poetry* (University of Arizona Press). In the fall he teaches Latinx poetry on the Notre Dame campus, and in the spring he teaches a poetry workshop in Washington, D.C. To learn more, visit: http://franciscoaragon.net

Michael Dowdy (foreword) is the author of *Broken Souths: Latina/o Poetic Responses to Neoliberalism and Globalization* (University of Arizona Press) and the co-editor, with Claudia Rankine, of *American Poets in the 21ˢᵗ Century: Poetics of Social Engagement* (Wesleyan University Press). As a poet, his works include a book, *Urbilly,* and a chapbook, *The Coriolis Effect*. He teaches at the University of South Carolina.

José Rodeiro (cover art) is a National Endowment for the Arts Visual Artist's Fellow; a Fulbright Scholar at University of Central America, Managua, Nicaragua, and a Cintas Fellow. His exhibits include Miami-Dade Museum of Art & Design, Monmouth Museum, Union City Museum, Museum of Fine Arts Washington County (Maryland), Mason Gross Gallery (Rutgers), Wilmer Jennings Gallery, Kenkeleba Gallery, New York State Arts Council Gallery (Manhattan), Florida International University's Frost Museum, Newark Museum, Galleries of Contemporary Art (Colorado Springs), UMDNJ's Robert Wood Johnson Gallery, Joyce Gordon Gallery, Perth Amboy Gallery, Ponce Museum (Puerto Rico), Maloney Gallery (Morristown, NJ).

Rubén's Friends

Deep gratitude to the patrons who, in part, made *After Rubén* possible—in particular its post publication promotion. ¡Gracias!

Anonymous (3)
Martha Aragon Velez
Tomás & Irene Aragón
Wally Babington
Kevin Baker
Ken Crocker
Hank Feenstra
Gary Hogle & Barbara Lahman
Steve Leahy
William McGrath
Steve McCarthy
José Medina
Kurt Mitchler
Paul Romero